Time-Sharing Systems

Consulting Editor

Professor D.W. Barron
University of Southampton

Other titles in the European Computer Science Series

Celia: An Introduction to Numerical Analysis
Meek: Algol by Problems
Shepherd: Algol 60 Programming

Time-Sharing Systems

G. M. Bull

S. F. G. Packham

McGRAW-HILL · LONDON

New York · St Louis · San Francisco · Düsseldorf
Johannesburg · Kuala Lumpur · Mexico · Montreal · New
Delhi · Panama · Rio de Janeiro · Singapore · Sydney
Toronto

Published by

McGRAW-HILL Book Company (UK) Limited

MAIDENHEAD · BERKSHIRE · ENGLAND

---

07 094161 0

Copyright © 1971 McGraw-Hill Book Company (UK) Limited.
All rights reserved. No part of this publication may be reproduced,
stored in a retrieval system, or transmitted, in any form or by any
means, electronic, mechanical, photocopying, recording, or otherwise,
without the prior permission of McGraw-Hill Book Company (UK)
Limited.

PRINTED AND BOUND IN GREAT BRITAIN

To Anne and Judith

Contents

Preface ix

Chapter 1 Introduction

1.1 Time-sharing 1
1.2 Historical background 3
1.3 Operating systems 5
1.4 Use and advantages of time-sharing 7

Chapter 2 User facilities

2.1 Command languages 10
2.2 Languages 19
2.3 Filing systems 25
2.4 Editors 28
2.5 Debugging aids 33
2.6 Terminal devices 38

Chapter 3 Methods of achieving time-sharing

3.1 Introduction 42
3.2 Remote job entry 42
3.3 Roll-in/roll-out job streams 46
3.4 Multiprogramming and swapping 52
3.5 Paging 57
3.6 Communications 60

Chapter 4 Design features

4.1 Interrupts and multiprogramming 66
4.2 Swapping and time-slices 74
4.3 Paging and segmentation 78
4.4 Re-entrant coding 86

4.5	Compilers and interpreters	89
4.6	System architecture	92
4.7	Multiplexers and communication processors	95

Chapter 5 *System management*

5.1	Resource allocation and control	103
5.2	Scheduling	106
5.3	System protection	111
5.4	Installation	113

Chapter 6 *Evaluation*

6.1	Benchmarking	117
6.2	Case study	121

Appendices	124
Bibliography	136
Index	139

Preface

The aim of this book is to try and bring together all the major aspects associated with the development of time-sharing systems, and the problems encountered with this evaluation. The impetus for this book stems largely from two sources. Firstly, in carrying out an evaluation we could find little literature that provided assistance in improving our understanding of the principles of time-sharing, or which gave guidance to assist us in making comparisons between the various systems. Secondly, the need for a text book to cover undergraduate courses in the subject. Much of the material in the book arises directly from our practical experiences in evaluating time-sharing systems. In order to carry out an evaluation exercise effectively, it is necessary to be aware of all the implications of both hardware and software system design. The book sets out to provide such a background. The material in the book is also based upon lecture material which has been successfully used for teaching at undergraduate level in computer science on courses similar to course I4 in the ACM Curriculum 68. The book covers almost all of the topics listed in course I4, including a number of those listed under 'other topics'. We hope therefore, that this book will prove useful to anyone (student or otherwise) who wishes to gain an understanding of time-sharing, as well as assisting those people who may be concerned with evaluating the possibilities of time-sharing within their operational environment.

There are many time-sharing systems in operation and almost as many attitudes and approaches to both implementation techniques and user facilities. Some systems provide but a single language, others many. Some offer excellent dynamic debugging facilities, others offer none. Some systems allow interaction at all stages—command level, file building and editing, compilation and execution—while on others the only interaction is the ability to supply data to the program at run time. Each system has its advantages and disadvantages, each has its market. The main emphasis in this book is on *highly interactive, multi-language, general-purpose time-sharing systems*, since it is this type of system which we set out to evaluate in practice.

The book is divided into six chapters, each of which represents a particular facet within the aims of the book.

Chapter 1 provides an introduction to the basic concepts of time-sharing, its relationship to the historical development of computer use and to operating system software upon which the success of time-sharing is so dependent.

Chapter 2 discusses the facilities that are available to the time-sharing user and includes a number of practical examples of these facilities in use.

Chapter 3 is concerned with methods by which time-sharing can be achieved. The chapter is subdivided into the major implementation methods in order that these may be more clearly defined.

Chapter 4 is an extension of the basic principles outlined in chapter 3. It is at a considerably more detailed level and can be bypassed without destroying the theme of the book.

Chapter 5 discusses the problems associated with system management, emphasizing the effect and importance of resource allocation and control, scheduling, system protection, and the problems of installation.

Chapter 6 is concerned with the practical problems of evaluation and includes a sample case study with documentation, representing one way in which the process of evaluation can be undertaken.

We wish to thank the many people who have helped us, including the various companies for their assistance in the production of the programming examples, Digital Equipment Corporation, International Computers Limited, and Dartmouth College for permission to quote from copyright material. Also our wives, Anne and Judith, without whom light relief would not have been possible. Finally, our special thanks are due to Dr R.W. Sharp, who led the evaluation team with such skill and good humour and provided constructive criticism of our final draft.

G.M. Bull
S.F.G. Packham

1 Introduction

> I always make the first verse well but I have a trouble in making the others.
>
> Molière

1.1 Time-sharing

Let us start by defining what we mean by the term 'time-sharing'. In current usage it can have one of two meanings. It can describe the use of different parts of the machine by different jobs being processed in the computer at the same time. This is *not* what we mean by time-sharing, and shall refer to this technique as 'multi-programming'; it should be noted that multi-programming is a very important technique used in many time-sharing systems, and is discussed in detail later. The second meaning of the term time-sharing, which we shall use, is the simultaneous interaction with a computer system by several users, each of whom is unaware of the presence of the others.

Much confusion had arisen over the difference between real-time and time-sharing operations. A 'real-time' system can be defined as one in which the time taken by the system to react to a particular input is sufficient to control the environment from which the input data originated. For example, let us consider a real-time airline seat reservation system. This clearly involves multiple simultaneous users (the booking clerks) and it is this factor which leads to the confusion. However, this type of system only gives the terminal operator access to a restricted number of highly specialized programs. There is no way for the terminal operator to write programs or to modify the suite of available programs; the terminal acts purely as an enquiry device. This is in no way compatible with the aims of time-sharing, which is to provide a readily available general computing facility. An alternative name for time-sharing is interactive or conversational computing.

Traditionally, jobs for the computer were transcribed onto say, punched cards, which were then transported to the computer room. The operator loaded the cards into the card reader and the job was processed, and the results of the run were typically printed out on a line printer. This stationery was then taken out of the computer room and distributed manually. The usual characteristics of this form of processing (batch processing) are that the user is not present at the run; he must specify in advance the action required under all foreseeable circumstances, and there is a considerable delay between submitting the job for processing and receiving the results of the run.

Under time-sharing, a user typically sits at a teletype which is connected to the central computer, either locally by a pair of wires or remotely using a common carrier facility (e.g., the switched public telephone network). The user is able to create and enter his job from the terminal and subsequently control its action by issuing commands appropriate to the response received at the terminal from the system. Should an error occur, the time-sharing user is able to make corrections to his program and rerun immediately. Although there may be many users carrying out similar operations at the same time, the time the system takes to respond to each user's commands and requests will be of the order of a few seconds. With virtually no delay between job runs, the time-sharing user is able to modify his job and achieve many runs during one session, thus reducing program development time. Further, and most importantly, the user is able to interact with his program while it is running. This new and powerful concept offers new avenues of approach to problem solving. For example, suppose we have set up a mathematical model of a physical situation and we wish to see the effects of changing the values of parameters. With time-sharing it is possible to make repeated changes, observe the effects, and then use human judgement to determine the next modification.

In order to see how it is possible to achieve time-sharing, let us consider the following over-simplified situation. Suppose a user at a terminal issues a command to the system which when obeyed occupies the computer for one-half of one second. If the user has to type 10 characters, at, say, an average speed of one character per second, then it takes the user 10 seconds to issue the command. During the typing of the command, the computer is doing work for this user for a negligible amount of time (say 0·000 05 seconds to accept each character as it is typed). Only on receiving notification of the end of the command string will the computer carry out the one-half second of computing. If there were only one user, the computer would be idle for most of the 10 seconds. If there were more than one user the idle time could be used by the computer to service the other users. It is clear that there is a limit to the number of users that a given computer can support. This is a function of the power of the computer, the type of work being undertaken by the users, and the length of time users are prepared to wait between issuing a command and that command being processed and completed. The last of these parameters is called the 'response time' of the system.

We have said earlier that each user is unaware of the presence of other users; he is thus given the illusion that he has sole use of the computer. It is clear that each user is not given the entire available resources of the machine for his own use. Each user is able to retain information on the system and have it filed by name on the backing store. It is clear, therefore, that the backing store must be shared by all users. We shall see later that other items, such as the main memory are also shared. Thus the computer which a user is working with is some subset of the actual computer.

1.2 Historical Background

In the early days of computing, each user had sole use of the machine while running his program and was both operator and programmer. This had the advantage for the programmer that he was able to run, check, correct, and run again immediately without frustrating time delays. However, this is an inefficient way of using the equipment, since the computer is idle for a great deal of time while the programmer considers the current state of his problem before he is able to take further action. As the demand for computers grew it became essential to eliminate inefficiencies in order to improve the total throughput on a given system. This led to the separation of the two jobs of operator and programmer. Machines were staffed by trained operators and the programmer no longer had direct access to the machine. Jobs were submitted to the operations staff with operating instructions. They were then sorted into batches of compatible jobs e.g., all programs written in the same programming language. This mode of operation led to the situation where a program was not necessarily run immediately following submission unless by chance it was placed in the next batch to be run. Since the programmer was not present at a run, he was no longer easily able to experiment with the program because there could be long delays between each run. As a result of this situation, he was forced to change his fault-finding (debugging) techniques. Before, he could make small changes at the machine and observe their effects immediately. With a long turn-around (the time between submission of the program and the receipt of the results), this natural mode of operation was no longer viable. In its place, he found himself spending considerable time deciphering octal core dumps (a print-out of the contents of the main memory following some error state)—a time-consuming and soul-destroying occupation. Thus, we have the position where the machine throughput has been dramatically increased at the expense of the programmer's facilities.

As the speed and capability of computers increased, it became necessary to remove decision-making processes from the operators, since they were no longer able to keep pace with the computer's processing power. Thus, batch-operating systems evolved which replaced many operator functions such as job scheduling and batching of similar tasks. Also, production jobs and frequently used programs were held on backing store within a structured filing system and hence it was no longer necessary to load the requisite programs manually at preset times. This achieved an improved machine throughput without giving the programmer any substantially better debugging facilities.

From the foregoing, we see that the man-machine interface was sadly neglected as a result of ther pressures. In the early 'sixties, the first time-sharing systems were implemented; the most notable of these experiments were carried out in two or three American universities.

Having outlined the natural development that has resulted in the establishment of time-sharing systems, we should now briefly consider the reasons for the somewhat delayed emergence of time-sharing systems in practice. There are two major factors which have operated against the rapid development and acceptance of time-sharing across a wide market.

Firstly, the largest market demand causes most computer manufacturers to tailor their machines to this market. The commercial, industrial, and government markets are of course the largest and it is these markets which indirectly have considerable influence over the characteristics exhibited by most computing equipment. Since the explosive expansion in the commercial use of computers started as late as the mid-sixties, it is hardly surprising that the buyers in this particular market are only now beginning to realize, and perhaps to have the time to consider, the advantages to be gained from using some form of time-sharing. Admittedly, in many cases, the requirements will not extend beyond a very restrictive form of interactive time-sharing, but nonetheless the need is now apparent. Since the demands of this market have been for large file-handling programs with restricted computation, it is not surprising that the impetus for time-sharing has come from the computer manufacturers outside this market. These manufacturers supplied the more obvious need for time-sharing in the scientific market, where program development and programs with a short life absorb much of the computing time. Thus, the large computer manufacturers have developed computers and software aimed towards their major market: large-scale batch processing. The most significant time-sharing systems, on the other hand, derived from the smaller specialist manufacturers supplying the scientific market. This market has had a more obvious need for the benefits to be derived from interactive time-sharing. It is unlikely that this situation will continue as the demands for time-sharing increases.

Secondly, there has always been a need for effective man-machine communication in all spheres of computing. Until recently, both the hardware and the software needed for time-sharing, and in particular the technology of data transmission, have not been in a viable and, more to the point, totally reliable state. Again, therefore, it is that section of the market which had the expertise and the will to experiment, namely the scientific/research sector which has made the most significant use of time-sharing. As a result of these efforts, time-sharing is now a reliable and effective method of using the computer, as is borne out by the rapid expansion in the number of time-sharing bureaux over the past few years.

Finally, both time-sharing and the general field of man-machine interaction will undoubtedly represent one of the major development areas in computer technology in the immediate future.

1.3 Operating Systems

The function of an operating system is to organize the work flow through a computer. In the case of batch processing, it is possible, but highly inefficient, to schedule work manually. In the case of time-sharing, manual control is not possible; it is only with suitable operating system software that we are able to achieve time-sharing. It is the time-sharing operating system software which enables a computer to communicate with, control, schedule, and respond within a short time to a number of simultaneous users, all of whom may be making varied demands upon the system such as manipulating files, compiling, editing, or running programs.

We can broadly classify operating systems into three categories—real-time, batch processing, and time-sharing. There are operating systems which do not fall into these categories—these are likely to be special-purpose systems—or which span more than one category. We can find a number of examples of the latter: a batch processing system which allows a simple and restricted form of time-sharing, time-sharing systems which allow simultaneous batch processing, a real-time system which provides time-sharing or batch processing simultaneously with real-time activity.

All operating systems, no matter what their overall function, have a number of characteristics in common. Operating systems handle all input and output operations. This is accomplished by a set of routines which we shall call the supervisor. (A number of terms are employed by various manufacturers for this suite of programs. A few examples are 'monitor', 'executive', and 'master'. Unfortunately, whereas one manufacturer uses, say, the word 'monitor' to describe the input–output routines and a number of associated routines for handling interrupts, another manufacturer will use the same term to describe the complete operating system.) Also, the operating system must arrange to schedule the varied use of the system resources. It must also control the resources of the system as efficiently as possible and in doing so may collect accounting data for use by system management. Another form of data collected by operating systems, useful to the designers of the system, particularly in the early stages of the use of the system, is the traffic of information within the system. A clear picture of the movement of data enables the designers to pinpoint bottlenecks, or potential bottlenecks, and modify the design to overcome this. One of the design aims of all operating systems is to reduce or eliminate real-time operator intervention. Finally, most operating systems maintain a filing system on-line.

Real-time systems. There are a number of examples of real-time systems in operation currently—airline seat reservation systems and the maintenance of customers' accounts by banks are two examples. Let us briefly consider an airline seat reservation system. The operating system has to handle a large number of enquiry terminals simultaneously, as well as any local peripherals such as line printers and backing store devices. If we simplify the situation and assume that there is a single program resident in main memory handling all enquiries and subsequent bookings, then the operating system is faced with the problem of scheduling the various enquiry terminals making use of the program. Since each enquiry is likely to take a number of minutes to complete, it is clear that the terminals must be handled in a similar fashion to those on a time-sharing system.

One design goal of a seat reservation system is total reliability, since the loss of all or part of the information could result in the total loss of business for the airline. (The banks face a similar problem.) To overcome this, all parts of the system are duplicated and all transactions are recorded twice, each on a different part of the system. Thus, a second processor and a second main memory are available should the first break down. It is possible to use this second machine to perform low-priority batch-processing tasks all the time it is not required. The batch work must be such that it can be suspended instantly, since the second processor and/or main memory must be available immediately the first breaks down. The batch processing work would run under a different operating system from that under which the real-time operating system runs.

Batch systems. The services a batch-processing operating system provides for both the user and the installation management are as follows.

The scheduling of jobs through the system as efficiently as possible with the minimum of real-time operator intervention. Techniques employed to achieve this include the use of a scheduling program (which takes into account such things as the demands on peripherals, main memory and files held on backing store, user-assigned priorities and deadlines, and maximum run times), multi-programming techniques, and spooling. Spooling is the mode of operation whereby output to slow devices, such as the line printer, is written to disc or tape to avoid delaying the program, since in general the output is generated by the program faster than the device can accept it. Later, or within the same multi-programming mix, the output is copied to the slow device. This technique may also be used for input. If all information necessary to run a job, including run-time data, is loaded into the system and retained on backing store in temporary files created by the operating system, a number of advantages may be realized. Operators are relieved of the task of loading the run-time data at the correct time, the scheduling program is able to run programs without regard to the availability or otherwise of slow peripherals, and programs are not held up by slow perpherals, thus enabling better use to be made of main memory since jobs will be inactive for less time.

The operating system dynamically controls the resources of the system—main memory peripherals, and central processor time. It also provides accounting information for effective management of the system. In the case of a bureau, charges are made for the use of the various parts of the system. It is the operating system which collects such information as the amount of memory used, the amount of processor time used, the number of cards read, the number of lines printed on the printer, and any other information needed. It may also operate a budgetary check to stop a customer (or in the case of an in-house machine, a department or other accounting unit) exceeding some measure of usage allocated to him.

A filing system held on backing store is administered by the operating system. In this filing system will be held such things as compilers, editors, loaders and other system programs, production programs, loaded jobs waiting to run under the control of the scheduling program, spooled data for various slow peripherals, and users' private information, typically programs and data. The maintenance of the system includes providing the user with facilities for adding new files, deleting old files, and generally manipulating files within his own directory for accessing them from a program as data, and for protecting the files from unauthorized use and system malfunction.

Time-sharing. A time-sharing operating system must provide facilities similar to those provided by a batch processing system. It must handle a number of terminals simultaneously, as well as all other peripherals. The scheduling of jobs through the system is vitally important and is approached with a view to maintaining an adequate response time for all users. The filing system must be made available to all terminal users simultaneously. The simultaneous use of the filing system makes the protection of users' files more important and more difficult. The files must also be protected against hardware and software failures. Most systems provide resource allocation, accounting, and budgeting facilities. Finally, and most importantly, a time-sharing operating system must provide each user with the ability to interact both with the system and with his own programs. To this end, a time-sharing system should have a particularly good user interface. That is, the user must not feel restricted by the functions provided by the operating system, nor should the functions make terminal operations difficult or tedious. Unhappily, this is not true of all time-sharing systems.

In summary we see that all three classes of operating systems have a number of functions in common. The differences in approach and solution are mainly a result of emphasis being placed upon different facets. Thus, in real-time operations the emphasis is on system integrity, response time, and the maintenance of a data base. In batch processing, the emphasis is upon efficient machine utilization and high throughput. In time-sharing, the emphasis is upon interaction and response time.

1.4 Use and Advantages of Time-sharing

The current uses and developments in time-sharing have mainly been in the fields of mathematics and statistics, technology, and education. This growth parallels the early usage of computers as outlined earlier. This is hardly surprising, as the early developments of computers and the more recent developments of time-sharing have both been initiated by universities and research laboratories. However, as has happened with the general use of computers, it is unlikely that this situation will continue for long, and we shall see the widespread use of some form of time-sharing in the commercial field.

The typical characteristics of a commercial program are its size and the amount of file activity involved. This is in direct contrast with the majority of 'scientific' programs. The initial implementations of time-sharing were on relatively small machines, which impeded commercial use. However, widespread awareness of the benefits of a large computing system to a commercial organization, together with the decreasing cost of computer power, has resulted in the installation of larger and more powerful computing systems. Many such systems have the characteristics which enable the implementation of at least simple time-sharing running concurrently with any batch activity. Thus, it would be surprising if the predictions about the large-scale use of time-sharing by commercial users is not realized in the near future.

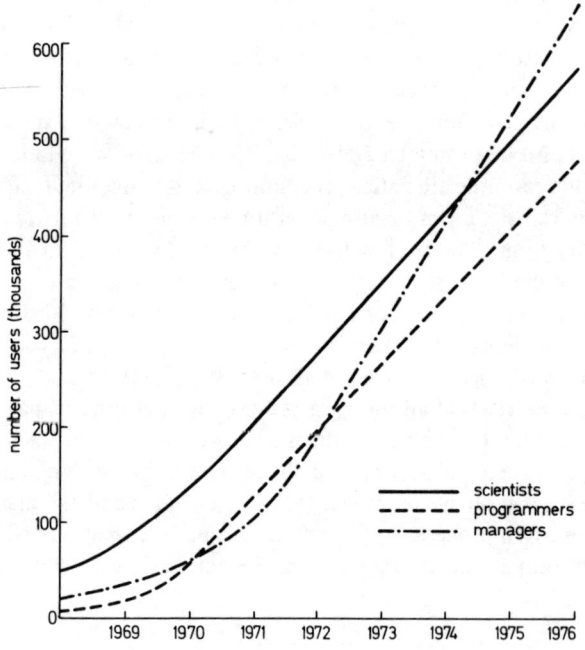

Fig. 1.1 Estimated prediction of the number of specified types of users of time-sharing in the U.S.A.

Figure 1.1 is a graph of predicted time-sharing use in the U.S.A. (not including remote batch processing) for specific types of users, and represents what we feel to be a reasonable extrapolation from figures currently available. It is only an estimation, but one which should give some idea of the possible expansion in the use of time-sharing facilities.

Finally, let us summarize some of the major advantages of time-sharing as follows:

(a) There is a substantial increase in the efficiency with which programs can be developed, tested and corrected.

(b) The facilities required to create, edit, compile, debug, and execute a program are available and may be used in a natural and efficient manner.

(c) The availability of time-sharing encourages programmers to be more inventive and imaginative in their approach to problem solving, since many ideas may be tried and modified in a short period of time.

(d) The computer is immediately available to all users from both remote and local sites. This availability has the effect of encouraging people for whom the computer is a tool to use the computer for tasks not previously tackled by them on a computer because of the frustrations of time delays or, more often, by the complexity of running programs under a batch-operating system and the need, very often, to use difficult batch programming languages. The last two points are particularly relevant, since time-sharing usually brings with it a simple to learn language such as JOSS or BASIC embedded in a simple operating system, which encourages people to make use of the system and apply it to their problem area.

(e) Time-sharing offers to the user the ability to interact both with the system and with his program, thereby enabling the user, for example, to guide the program from the terminal as it is running.

(f) Time-sharing allows users to easily communicate ideas and information (e.g., via the filing system) to other users of the system, with the obvious advantage that work is not duplicated, new ideas and methods are disseminated among the users, and information is centralized.

(g) Time-sharing makes available to the casual user facilities which, if offered in a batch processing environment, would be under the exclusive control of professional programmers.

In the past, there has been the design concept (in both hardware and software) of running a program in a computer with little or no communication with the outside world, other than a few messages to the operator. With the advent of time-sharing this is considered incomplete. It is now essential to consider man-machine interation in the solution of a problem.

2 User Facilities

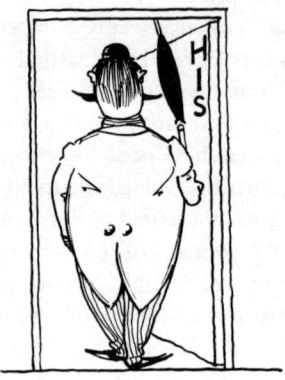

2.1 Command Languages

When using a time-sharing system, we wish to make use of a number of different system programs which provide us with a variety of services. For example, we make use of compilers to translate source programs into object programs, editors to correct and modify source programs, debugging aids to correct and modify object programs, and a number of other utility programs to perform such tasks as loading binary programs into main memory, and manipulating data within the filing system. To gain access to these systems programs, we must communicate with the operating system by means of instructions to tell the (operating) system what to do next on our behalf. The set of instructions available for this purpose is called the command language.

In contrast with the case of programming languages, there has been little attempt to standardize command languages, with the result that each system has its own command language with its own conventions.

Commands may be classified into a number of categories. Not all time-sharing systems have commands in all categories; for example, not all time-sharing systems allow a background (low-priority batch processing) stream, not all systems allow users to allocate facilities to themselves such as magnetic tape units, line printers, etc. The categories of commands are:

    (a)   system access,
    (b)   editing,

(c) file manipulation,
(d) compiling and executing,
(e) background job control,
(f) system administration, and
(g) resource allocation.

The commands that are typically available under these seven categories are as follows:

(a) System access. Usually, there are just two commands, one to gain access to the system (logging in) and one to terminate operations at the end of a session at the terminal (logging out). Security at login time will be discussed under filing systems.

(b) Editing. We shall discuss editors in more detail later. Editors either use a line as the basic unit (line editors) or operate on strings of characters (text editors). It is usual to make use of an editor to create source programs. Some systems provide a few line-editing functions as commands rather than as part of a separate Editor.

(c) File manipulation. Under this category, we have commands to create new files in the filing system, delete files no longer required, list the contents of source files, change the names of files, list the names of the files in our directory of personal files, and access files previously created and saved.

(d) Compiling and executing. Here we are concerned with commands which may do many jobs such as compile, load the object program into main memory, and then cause the program to be executed, or which may do only one of the above steps. In general, we have commands to compile, load, execute, to halt a running program, and continue after a halt. This last command is only useful if we can take meaningful action following a halt, before setting the program running again.

(e) Background job control. Some time-sharing systems allow users to create jobs at a terminal and either to enter the job into a background batch processing stream or to set the job running and then 'detach' the terminal from the job so that the terminal may then be used for some other purpose. Obviously, we cannot run a job in this manner if it requests input from the terminal or wishes to output results to the terminal while running. The commands required will depend upon the method of implementation, but will include commands to run the job in the background mode, to reconnect at some time later, and to interrogate the system for a progress report on the job at any stage.

(f) System administration. Many of these commands may only be available to the operators and issuable only from the operator's console. However, some systems allow the user to gain information about such things as the numbers of users currently logged-in, the time of day, and the status of one's account. On some systems, it is possible to send messages to the operator to request some action from him such as loading a deck of cards or mounting a magnetic tape. On some systems, this is extended to allow you to send and receive messages from any other user on the system who is logged-in and willing to talk to you.

(g) Resource allocation. In some time-sharing systems, all the facilities of the system are administered by the system. In others, parts of the system are made available to users and in this case commands will be required to facilitate this. The commands provide the ability to assign and release various peripherals, allocate and deallocate main memory, and the ability to print out the availability of resources.

Of the above, all systems have commands in the first four categories in that they are fundamental to time-sharing.

Commands may be further classified according to the demands which they make upon the system. File building—typing in a program, for example—is an operation that makes only trivial demands on the system. Compilation, on the other hand, makes non-tirivial demands. As we should expect, those commands requiring little work by the system are dealt with more quickly than those requiring considerable work. Thus, we should expect to be able to type in a program as fast as we can type, whereas it is not unreasonable to expect a *small* delay following a compile command. The time delay experienced at various points in the 'conversation' with the system is termed the 'response time'. We shall see that a number of factors other than the particular command determine the response time—the configuration, the method of implementation, the activity of other users at the time, and the scheduling algorithm.

To give some idea of the range of command formats, let us now look at a few examples. We shall set out in all cases to type in a simple FORTRAN program, compile the program, make corrections to the source program as a result of error messages received from the compiler, list the new version of the program, compile this new program, and then run the program. All computer output is underlined (for single lines) or enclosed in brackets (for multiple lines). We shall adopt this notation in all examples throughout the book.

```
↑C                              enter monitor mode to issue commands
. LOGIN                         the period tells us we may type a command
JOB 10         DEC PDP 10 10/50 MONITOR
≠10,66
PASSWORD:                       user identification
2157 11-FEB-70 TTY22
↑C                              system tells us we are still in monitor mode
. CREATE FTEST                  create a new file called FTEST using the
                                editor
*I10,10                         edit command to insert lines from line number
                                10 in steps of 10
00010          INTEGER CENTS,DOLL,HALF,QTR,DIME,NKL,CT
00020    C     THIS PROGRAM PRINTS A COIN ANALYSIS IN DOLLARS
00030    C     HALFS,QUARTERS,DIMES,NICKELS AND CENTS FOR A
00040    C     GIVEN NUMBER OF CENTS SUPPLIED BY THE USER
00050          ACCEPT 10,CENTS
00060          DOLL=CENTS/100
00070          CT=CENTS-DOLL*100
```

12

00080	HALF=CT/50	
00090	CT=CT-HALF*50	type in FORTRAN program, the line numbers
00100	QTF\F\R=CT/25	are supplied by the editor as a result of the
00120	DIME=CT/10	command I10,10 above example of character
00130	CT=CT-DIME*10	deleting (F) in line 100
00140	NKL-CT/5	
00150	CT=CT-NKL*5	
00160	TYPE 20,DOLL,HALF,QTR,DIME,NKL,CT	
00170	FORMAT(I6)	
00180	FORMAT(6I5)	
00190	END	
00200 $		exit from file building, end of file in line 190.
*E		the * tells us we may type an edit command, in this case exit from editor and return to monitor mode.

*↑C
. EXECUTE FTEST   execute (i.e. compile, load and enter) FTEST

```
        00140 NKL-CT/5              compiler error messages point to an error in
                ↑                   line 140 (the - should be an =) and two labels,
        S-1 SYNTAX                  10 and 20, are used in the program (lines 50
                                    and 160) but not supplied elsewhere.
UNDEFINED LBLS

20
10
MAIN.   ERRORS DETECTED: 3

? TOTAL ERRORS DETECTED: 3          had these been subprograms this total might
                                    have been more meaningful

2K CORE USED                        not usually of interest to the general user
```

*↑C   exit from the compiler and return to monitor
                                     mode — no execution as there were errors.
. EDIT   re-enter the editor

*I140
00140   NKL=CT/5   change lines 140, 170 and 180
ILR   the *ILR* messages have no significance
*I170   to those edit commands but are useful in
                                     other cases.

00170   10   FORMAT(I6)
ILR
*I180
00180   20   FORMAT(6I5)
ILR
*P10,190   ask the editor to print lines 10 through 190

   listing of correct program
*E   exit to monitor mode

*↑C

. EXECUTE   execute FTEST again

13

MAIN. ERRORS DETECTED: 0	no errors this time
2K CORE USED	
LOADER 4+2K CORE	loading takes place after compilation
EXIT	exit from loader
↑C	
567	program running — supply data for the ACCEPT statement
5 1 0 1 1 2	results produced by line 160
EXIT	exit from execution
↑C	
.	back in monitor mode and we may issue further commands.

!BTM ON SIGMA 5	the ! tells us we are in monitor mode
10/02/'70 15: 11	
!LOGIN: ACC1,SDS,6005	user identification
ID=C	
!TABS 7,72	set tab stops to columns 7 and 72 for FORTRAN layout
!EDIT	call in the editor
*BUILD FTEST	create a new file called FTEST using the editor

Line	Code	Comment
1.000	INTEGER CENTS,DOLL,HALF,QTR,DIME,NKL,CT	
2.000	C THIS PROGRAM PRINTS A COIN ANALYSIS IN DOLLARS,	
3.000	C HALFS,QUARTERS,DIMES,NICKELS AND CENTS FOR A	
4.000	C GIVEN NUMBER OF CENTS SUPPLIED BY THE USER	
5.000	READ (6,10) CENTS	
6.000	DOLL=CENTS/100	
7.000	CT=CENTS-DOLL*100	
8.000	HALF=CT/50	type in FORTRAN program
9.000	CT=CT-HALF*50	the line numbers are supplied by the
10.000	QTF←R=CT/25	editor, the tab key is used to get to
11.000	CT=CT-QTR*25	column seven
12.000	DIME=CT/10	example of character deleting (F) in
13.000	CT=CT-DIME*10	line 10
14.000	NKL-CT/5	
15.000	CT=CT-NKL*5	
16.000	WRITE (6,20) DOLL,HALF,QTR,DIME,NKL,CT	
17.000	FORMAT(I6)	
18.000	FORMAT(6I5)	
19.000	END	
20.000		exit from file building, end of file in line 19

*END	exit from editor to monitor mode
!ASSIGN M:SI, (FILE,FTEST)	assign the file FTEST as source input (SI)
!FORTRAN	call in the FORTRAN compiler
OPTIONS: BO	ask for a binary output file

```
    14:    NKL-CT/5
                ↑
```

**** SYNTAX	compiler error messages point to an error in line 14 (the - should be an =) and
**** LABEL ERRORS	some label errors
** END OF COMPILATION **	exit from the compiler to monitor mode.

14

!EDIT					re-enter the editor, the * tells us we may give an edit command
*EDIT FTEST					tell the editor that we wish to edit FTEST
*IN 14					
14.000		NKL=CT/5			
*IN 17					
17.000	10	FORMAT(I6)			change lines 14, 17 and 18
*IN 18					
18.000	20	FORMAT(6I5)			
*END					exit from the editor to monitor mode
!FERRET					call in file management system
≥E FTEST					> tells us we can give a FERRET command, in this case Examine
#					# invites us to provide options, giving none implies examine the entire file
listing of correct program					
≥X					exit from FERRET to monitor mode
!FORTRAN					call the FORTRAN compiler
OPTIONS: BO					ask for a binary output file
** END OF COMPILATION **					no errors this time
!LOAD					call the loader
ELEMENT FILES:					
OPTIONS:					take standard options
F:6					6 relates to the 6 in the READ and WRITE statements in lines 5 and 16, we have indicated that device 6 is to be our teletype
F;					
SEV.LEV. = 0					no loader errors
XEQ? Y					we wish to execute the program — it is now running input data for the READ statement results produced by line 16
: 567					
5	1	0	1	1 2	
STOP					
USER EXIT.					exit from execution to monitor mode
!					back in monitor mode and we may issue further commands.

G.E.I.S. LTD.

ON AT 14:25   GEIS B 25/02/70   TTY22

USER NUMBER--B968,36	user identification
PROJECT ID--BOOK	accounting information
SYSTEM--FORTRAN	tell the system we are using FORTRAN
NEW OR OLD--NEW	create a new file
NEW FILE NAME--FTEST	call it FTEST
READY.	

```
10          INTEGER CENTS,DOLL,HALF,QTR,DIME,NKL,CT
20C         THIS PROGRAM PRINTS A COIN ANALYSIS IN DOLLARS
30C         HALFS,QUARTERS,DIMES,NICKELS AND CENTS FOR A
40C         GIVEN NUMBER OF CENTS SUPPLIED BY THE USER
```

15

50	INPUT 10,CENTS	
60	DOLL=CENTS/100	
70	CT=CENTS-DOLL*100	
80	HALF=CT/50	type in FORTRAN program the line
90	CT=CT-HALF*50	numbers are supplied by the user and
100	QTF←R=CT/25	may be in any order the system will
110	CT=CT-QTR*25	sort them into order
120	DIME=CT/10	example of character deleting (F) in
130	CT=CT-DIME*10	line 100
140	NKL-CT/5	
150	CT=CT-NKL*5	
160	PRINT 20,DOLL,HALF,QTR,DIME,NKL,CT	
170	FORMAT(I6)	
180	FORMAT(6I5)	
190	END	
RUN		run (i.e. compile, load and execute) FTEST, the system recognises a command by the absence of a line number

```
⎡FTEST    14:    GEIS B 25/02/70
 140       NKL-CT/5
 NOT A STMT.---------↑
 AT LINE NO. 190, 10: IS UNDEF.
 AT LINE NO. 190, 20: IS UNDEF.

 ERRORS, NO EXEC.

⎣USED          2.33 SEC.
```

compiler error messages point to an error in line 140 (the - should be an =) and two labels, 10 and 20, are used in the program (lines 50 and 160) but not supplied

No execution as these were errors

2.33 seconds of central processor time used

140		NKL=CT/5
170	10	FORMAT(I6)
180	20	FORMAT(6I5)
LIST		

change lines 140, 170 and 180

list the program

listing of correct program

RUN   run FTEST again

FTEST   14:33   GEIS B 25/02/70

```
? 567
⎡
   5   1   0   1   1   2
 AT LINE NO. 190: STOP END
⎣USED    5.33 SEC
```

the ? is a request for data from the INPUT statement in line 50

results produced by line 160

exit from program

ON AT 11:32   04/02/70   THURSDAY   LDN LINE 18
WELCOME TO CALL/360
USER NUMBER,PASSWORD--CAA25,SOFTWARE   user identification
<u>READY</u>

ENTER FORTRAN
<u>READY</u>   tell the system we are using FORTRAN

```
NAME FTEST
READY                           create a new file called FTEST
  10  INTEGER CENTS,DOLL,HALF,QTR,DIME,NKL,CT
  20  READ(5,10)CENTS
  30  DOLL=CENTS/100
  40  CT=CENTS-DOLL*100          type in FORTRAN program
  50  HALF=CT/50                 the line numbers are supplied by the
  70  QTF                        user and may be in any order, the
      R=CT/25                    system will sort them into order
  80  CT=CT-QTR*25               example of character deleting
  90  DIME=CT/10                 (F) in line 70
 100  CT=CT-DIME*10
 110  NKL-CT/5
 120  CT=CT-NKL*5
 130  WRITE(6,20) DOLL,HALF,QTR,DIME,NKL,CT
 140  FORMAT(I6)
 150  FORMAT(6I5)
 160  STOP
 170  END
RUN                             run (i.e. compile, load and execute)
                                FTEST

FTEST   11:40  04/02/70   THURSDAY   LDN

LINE 110 SYNTAX ERROR           compiler error messages point to an
                                error in line 110 (the - should be an =)
                                and two labels, 10 and 20, are used in
LABLING ERRORS                  the program (lines 20 and 130) but not
                                supplied.
 10
 20
SEVERE ERRORS EXECUTION INHIBITED
                                no execution as there were errors
TIME    1 SECS.                 1 second of central processor time

 110  NKL=CT/5
 140  10 FORMAT(I6)
 150  20 FORMAT(6I5)             change lines 110, 140 and 150
LIST                            list the program

listing of correct program

RUN                             run FTEST again

FTEST   11:42  04/02/70   THURSDAY   LDN

? 456                           the ? is a request for data from the
                                READ statement in line 20

    4   1   0   0   1   1       results produced by line 130
STOP                            exit from program
TIME    1 SECS.
```

M.0076 HELLO...RTS IS ON THE AIR.   DATE 04/01/70
M.0078 THE TIME IS 1644 HOURS. ENTER '/ID CONTRACT'.
■/ID   overscored user identification
M.0155 IN THE CASE OF RESTART. ENTER '/RESTART CONTRACT,008.'

```
GO
≥/INPUT                                 create a file
≥/JOB GO                                compile and execute
≥/FTC                                   use the FORTRAN compiler
≥        INTEGER CENTS,DOLL,HALF,QTR,DIME,NKL,CT
≥        READ(9,10) CENTS
≥        DOLL=CENTS/100
≥        CT=CENTS-DOLL*100              type in FORTRAN program
≥        HALF=CT/50                     example of character deleting
≥        CT=CT-HALF*50                  (F) in the eighth line of
≥        CT=CT-QTF←R*25                 FORTRAN code.
≥        DIME=CT/10
≥        CT=CT-DIME*10
≥        NKL-CT/5
≥        CT=CT-NKL*5
≥        WRITE(7,20) DOLL,HALF,QTR,DIME,NKL,CT
≥        FORMAT(I6)
≥        FORMAT(6I5)
≥        STOP
≥        END
≥/ENDRUN                                end of file building, run program
   0011           NKL-CT/5
                  $
          01) IEY0131 SYNTAX            compiler error messages point to an
   0014           FORMAT(I6)            error in line 11 of the program and
                  $                     two labels errors associated with lines
          01) IEY0021 LABEL             14 and 15.
   0015           FORMAT(6I5)           There are two undefined labels 10 and
                  $                     20.
          01) IEY0021 LABEL             for a full explaination of each error the
                                        manual may be consulted and the error
                                        code (e.g. IEY0131) used to obtain
                                        more help.

                  IEY0221    UNDEFINED LABEL
      10    20

MAIN   MEMORY REQS (BYTES) 0001EA HEX    00490 DEC   space required.
IHC2301-SOURCE ERROR AT ISN 00002-@EXECUTION FAILED AT SUBROUTINE
MAIN

TIME:     3.340 SECS.                   inspite of compile time errors
OK                                      execution is attempted.
GO
≥/UPDATE                                open file for editing
≥/CHANGE 13,13                          change line 13 (the two commands are part
≥        NKL=CT/5                       of the file so this refers to the eleventh
                                        line of FORTRAN)
≥/CHANGE 16,17                          change lines 16 and 17
≥     10 FORMAT(I6)
≥     20 FORMAT(6I5)
≥/END                                   end of edit

OK
GO                                      list the file
```

```
≥/DISPLAY
L.0001  /JOB GO
L.0002  /FTC
L.0003          INTEGER CENTS,DOLL,HALF,QTR,DIME,NKL,CT
L.0004          READ(9,10) CENTS    device 9 is input from the terminal
L.0005          DOLL=CENTS/100
L.0006          CT=CENTS-DOLL*100
L.0007          HALF=CT/50
L.0008          CT=CT-HALF*50
L.0009          QTR=CT/25
L.0010          CT=CT-QTR*25
L.0011          DIME=CT/10
L.0012          CT=CT-DIME*10
L.0013          NKL=CT/5
L.0014          CT=CT-NKL*5
L.0015          WRITE(7,20) DOLL,HALF,QTR,DIME,NKL,CT
                                device 7 is output to terminal
L.0016       10 FORMAT(I6)
L.0017       20 FORMAT(6I5)
L.0018          STOP
L.0019          END
L.0020  /ENDRUN
OK
GO
≥/XEQ                           execute the program
MAIN    MEMORY REQS (BYTES) 00023A HEX    000570 DEC
≥  456                          data for the READ statement
   4    1   0   0   1   1       results from the WRITE statement
IHC0021 STOP    0               exit
TIME:   2.880 SECS.             2.880 seconds of central processor time
OK
GO
≥
```

2.2 Languages

Most programming languages in use today were designed for off-line, batch processing. To be more precise, they were not designed for on-line interactive work. Most off-line languages can be adapted for use on-line with varying success. Since programs are entered from the terminal, one does not want to use a language with causes a great deal of typing, particularly if some less verbose language, suitable for solving the problem, is available. Thus, for example, very little use is made of COBOL on-line. This is for two reasons. Firstly, COBOL is not an ideal on-line language, and, secondly, time-sharing has so far had more impact in science, engineering, and education than in the commercial world. This is changing, and COBOL is available on a number of systems. It may well be that a commercial language designed for on-line use will appear in the near future.

As we have stressed earlier, the major advantage to the user of time-sharing is the ability to debug programs more easily and efficiently. As a general rule, a user finds it easier to debug if the language he is using is of the form where there is one statement per line. Thus, for example, FORTRAN-like languages (leaving aside continuation statements) adapt to on-line use rather more easily than ALGOL or COBOL-like languages. The reasons underlying this statement will become clearer when we discuss debugging in detail later.

Although it is possible to adapt languages for use on-line (reference the FORTRAN examples), it is usual that the full benefits of time-sharing are more easily and (therefore) more often realized using a language developed for interactive on-line use. We shall consider two such languages in common use. The first, JOSS, was developed for use by scientists and engineers at the Rand Corporation and has been in daily use there and elsewhere since January 1964. The language is available on a number of systems under a number of names: AID, CAL, CITRAN, ESI, FIGARO, ISIS, PIL/I, JEAN, and TELCOMP, among others. The stated goal of the original experiment was to demonstrate the value of on-line access to a computer via an appropriate language, designed to give the individual scientist or engineer an easy, direct way of solving small numerical problems. It has unquestionably fulfilled this aim.

```
. R AID
AID (14-MAR-69) AT YOUR SERVICE...
*AID IS THE VERSION OF JOSS AVAILABLE ON THE*
*DEC PDP10. THE ASTERISK AT THE BEGINNING OF*
*EACH LINE IS TO TELL US WHEN WE MAY TYPE. AN*
*ASTERISK AT THE END OF THE LINE CAUSES THE*
*LINE TO BE IGNORED. THIS FACILITY MAY BE USED*
*TO PRODUCE COMMENTARY. AS HERE. OR TO DELETE*
*AN INCORRECT LINE. AID MAY BE USED AS A "DESK*
*CALCULATOR" USING TYPE. ALL STEPS ARE*
*TERMINATED BY A PERIOD OR AN ASTERISK*
*TYPE 6*4.
          6*4=    24
*WE MAY STORE VALUES FOR LATER USE USING SIMPLE VARIABLES*
*SET A=4.
*TYPE SQRT(A).
          SQRT(A)=    2
*SET P=50
*SET R=4.5.
*SET T=4.5.
*WE MAY USE THESE VALUES TO ASSIGN A VALUE TO ANOTHER
VARIABLE*
*LET I=(P*R*T)/100.
*TYPE I.
          I =     6.75
*WE CAN DESCRIBE THE FORMAT OF THE OUTPUT*
*FORM 1:
*I= ←← . ←←←←
*TYPE I IN FORM 1.
   I= 6.7500
*FORMS MAY BE USED TO OUTPUT TEXT*
*FORM 4:
```

∗THIS IS A TEXT OUTPUT
∗TYPE FORM 4.
THIS IS A TEXT OUTPUT
∗IT IS POSSIBLE TO STORE STEPS FOR LATER EXECUTION∗
∗1.1 SET L=6.5.
∗1.2 SET D=L∗2.4.
∗1.3 TYPE L,D.
∗STEPS ARE ORGANISED INTO PARTS ACCORDING TO THE INTEGER∗
∗PORTION OF THEIR STEP NUMBERS. THUS WE MAY EXECUTE∗
∗THE ABOVE STEPS BY TYPING:∗
∗DO PART 1.
```
        L =       6.5
        D =      15.6
```
∗WE MAY MAKE CHANGES - INSERT NEW STEPS. DELETE OR REPLACE∗
∗OLD STEPS. FOR EXAMPLE: ∗
∗1.3 TYPE L,D IN FORM 2.
∗THIS VERSION OF 1.3 HAS REPLACED THE OLD STEP 1.3∗
∗WE MAY ASK TO SEE A COPY OF STEP 1.3∗
∗TYPE STEP 1.3.
 1.3 TYPE L,D IN FORM 2.
∗DO PART 1.
ERROR AT STEP 1.3: I CAN'T FIND THE REQUIRED FORM.
∗FORM 2:
∗←←.←← CONVERTS TO .
∗GO.
   6.50 CONVERTS TO   15.60
∗VARIOUS ITEMS CAN BE DISPLAYED IN THIS WAY SUCH AS THE∗
∗INDIVIDUAL STEPS,PARTS,ALL THE PROGRAM,VALUES OF ∗
∗VARIABLES (ALL OR INDIVIDUALLY), FORMS ETC.∗
∗TYPE ALL VALUES.
```
        A =       4
        D =      15.6
        L =       6.5
        P =      50
        R =       4.5
        T =       3
```
∗TYPE PART 1.
 1.1 SET L=6.5.
 1.2 SET D=L∗2.4.
 1.3 TYPE L,D IN FORM 2.
∗IT IS POSSIBLE FOR US TO INTERACT WITH A PROGRAM BY∗
∗SUPPLYING DATA AT RUN TIME USING "DEMAND"∗
∗2.1 DEMAND X.
∗DO STEP 2.1.
          X = ∗3
∗TYPE X.
          X =   3
∗1.1 DEMAND L.
∗TYPE PART 1.
 1.1 DEMAND L.
 1.2 SET D=L∗2.4.
 1.3 TYPE L,D IN FORM 2
∗1.4 TO STEP 1.1.

*DO PART 1.
   L =   *6.5
 6.50 CONVERTS TO 15.60
   L =   *2
 2.00 CONVERTS TO 4.80
   L = *
I'M AT STEP 1.1.
*CANCEL.
THE CHARACTER "RETURN" TERMINATES INTERACTION
AN ALTERNATIVE FORM OF THE DEMAND STATEMENT IS
*1.1 DEMAND L AS 'NUMBER OF POUNDS".
*DO PART 1.
    NUMBER OF POUNDS = *2
 2.00 CONVERTS TO 4.80
   NUMBER OF POUNDS = *
*I'M AT STEP 1.1.
*CANCEL.
ERRORS ARE DIAGNOSED AND CORRECTED IN A NUMBER OF WAYS
*TYPE H.
H = ???
*SET H=2.
*TYPE H.
   H =   2
*3.1 TYPD\D\E X.
*TYPE STEP 3.1.
3.1 TYPE X.
THE "RUBOUT" KEY IS USED TO DELETE A CHARACTER
THE SYSTEM ECHOES A BACK SLASH FOLLOWED BY THE
DELETED CHARACTER. ANY FURTHER RUBOUTS WILL ECHO AS
THE NEXT DELETED CHARACTER. WHEN A NON-RUBOUT CHARACTER
IS MET A BACK SLASH IS TYPED BY THE SYSTEM TO ENCLOSE
THE DELETED STRING OF CHARACTERS. IN THE ABOVE EXAMPLE
WE HAVE DELETED THE SINGLE CHARACTER D
*DELETE ALL.
THIS CLEARS THE SLATE. WE SHALL NOW WRITE A PROGRAM
TO DO TAX CALCULATIONS (UK STYLE!)
*1.1 DEMAND G AS "GROSS ANNUAL PAY =".
*1.2 DEMAND A AS "TOTAL ALLOWANCES =".
*1.3 LET N=G-A.
*1.4 TO PART 2 IF N<100.
*1.5 SET T=20.
FIRST 100 TAXABLE AT 4/- IN THE POUND
*1.6 LET N=N-100.
*1.7 TO PART 3 IF N<200.
*1.8 LET N=N-200.
*1.9 SET T=80.
NEXT 200 AT 6/- IN THE POUND GIVING TOTAL OF 80
*1.95 LET T=T+N*8.25/20.
*1.96 TO PART 4.
REST TAXABLE AT 8/3 IN THE POUND
*2.1 LET T=N*0.2.
*2.2 TO PART 4.
*3.1 LET T=T+N*0.3.

```
*3.2 TO PART 4.
*4.1 TYPE T IN FORM 1.
*FORM 1:
*TOTAL TAX PAYABLE =
*DO PART 1.
        GROSS ANNUAL PAY = *5000
        TOTAL ALLOWANCES = *1000
TOTAL TAX PAYABLE = 1606.25
*DELETE ALL.
*↑C
*
```

The second language we shall look at is BASIC, developed at Dartmouth College primarily for undergraduate use. It is a simple language to learn and yet very powerful. Since 1965 it has grown, and continues to grow, from a limited language to one which gives the programmer many powerful facilities. Unlike most general purpose off-line languages it incorporates within it facilities for reading and writing files, instructions for communicating directly with the user, the ability to communicate between two programs as well as such things as matrix instructions and character handling capabilities. As part of the BASIC system, there exists a well-defined set of commands and editing functions which make the use of the system as convenient as possible. An example of a BASIC program is given below.

```
SYSTEM--BASIC
NEW OR OLD--NEW
NEW FILE NAME--MONEY
READY.

100 PRINT
110 REMARK A PRINT ON ITS OWN CAUSES A NEW LINE TO BE THROWN
120 PRINT "THIS PROGRAM CALCULATES THE AMOUNT OF MONEY THAT"
130 PRINT "WOULD ACCUMULATE AFTER N YEARS AT AN ANNUAL INTERES'
140 PRINT "RATE R COMPOUNDED T TIMES PER YEAR, WHEN THE INITIAL"
150 PRINT "CAPITAL IS P AND AN AMOUNT D IS ADDED AT THE BEGINNING"
160 PRINT "OF EACH SUBSEQUENT YEAR. P AND D ARE IN DOLLARS, N AND
170 PRINT "MUST BE INTEGRAL AND R IS GIVEN AS A PERCENTAGE."
180 PRINT
190 PRINT 'WHAT ARE P,D,N,T,AND R';
200 INPUT P,D,N,T,R
205 REMARK THIS CALLS FOR THE FIVE VALUES AT RUN TIME
210 IF T<>0 THEN 250
220 PRINT
230 PRINT "T MUST BE NON ZERO"
240 GOTO 190
250 LET B=0.1*R
260 LET S=P
270 LET X=0
280 FOR Z=1 TO N
290 LET S=S+X
300 FOR W=1 TO T
```

```
310 LET S=S*(1+B/T)
320 NEXT W
330 LET X=D
340 NEXT Z
350 PRINT
360 PRINT "AFTER";N;"YEARS, ";P;"DOLLARS INVESTED AT";R
370 PRINT "PERCENT COMPOUNDED ";T;"TIMES PER YEAR, WITH THE"
380 PRINT "ADDITION OF ";D;"DOLLARS PER YEAR, YIELDS A TOTAL"
390 PRINT "OF ";S;"DOLLARS."
400 PRINT
410 PRINT "AGAIN - YES OR NO";
420 INPUT A$
430 REMARK A$ IS A STRING VARIABLE AND THIS CALLS FOR "YES" OR "NO"
435 REMARK AS INPUT RATHER THAN FOR A NUMBER
440 IF A$ = "YES" THEN 190
500 END
RUN
```

MONEY   15:41

THIS PROGRAM CALCULATES THE AMOUNT OF MONEY THAT
WOULD ACCUMULATE AFTER N YEARS AT AN ANNUAL INTEREST
RATE R COMPOUNDED T TIMES PER YEAR. WHEN THE INITIAL
CAPITAL P AND AN AMOUNT D IS ADDED AT THE BEGINNING
OF EACH SUBSEQUENT YEAR. P AND D ARE IN DOLLARS, N AND T
MUST BE INTEGRAL AND R IS GIVEN AS A PERCENTAGE.

WHAT ARE P,D,N,T,AND R?   1000,100,10,12,1

AFTER 10 YEARS, 1000 DOLLARS INVESTED AT 1
PERCENT COMPOUNDED 12 TIMES PER YEAR, WITH THE
ADDITION OF 100 DOLLARS PER YEAR, YIELDS A TOTAL
OF 4237.25 DOLLARS.

AGAIN - YES OR NO? YES

WHAT ARE P,D,N,T,AND R? 100,100,10,12,1

AFTER 10 YEARS, 100 DOLLARS INVESTED AT 1
PERCENT COMPOUNDED 12 TIMES PER YEAR, WITH THE
ADDITION OF 100 DOLLARS PER YEAR, YIELD A TOTAL
OF 1800.91 DOLLARS.

AGAIN - YES OR NO? NO

USED   10.50 SEC.

Most time-sharing systems offer the user a range of languages at the terminal. A not uncommon combination of languages is the assembly language of the particular machine, FORTRAN and BASIC. In evaluating a system, we must obviously consider the availability of languages at the terminal, but, all other things being equal, it is far more important to evaluate the debugging aids available with the languages than any other language feature. Some systems make use of compilers written for a batch-operating system, and as a result most of the important facilities are missing.

2.3 Filing Systems

Information held on-line by a system for its users is organized into files. A file is simply an ordered sequence of information items such as a program, data, a list of the names of other files in the filing system, and in fact anything which the user cares to keep on the system. The files together constitute the filing system which is held on backing-store devices such as drums, discs, and magnetic tapes. We shall distinguish between two types of files—those which are directories and contain information about other files within the filing system, and those which are not directories. Information about a user's files is kept in a directory belonging to that user. This directory will contain information about each of the user's files, such as the name of the file, date and time of creation, date and time of last access, and where the file is currently held within the backing-store. Also held within the directory will be security information such as passwords, names of users allowed to access the file other than the owner, and the type of access each of the listed users is allowed.

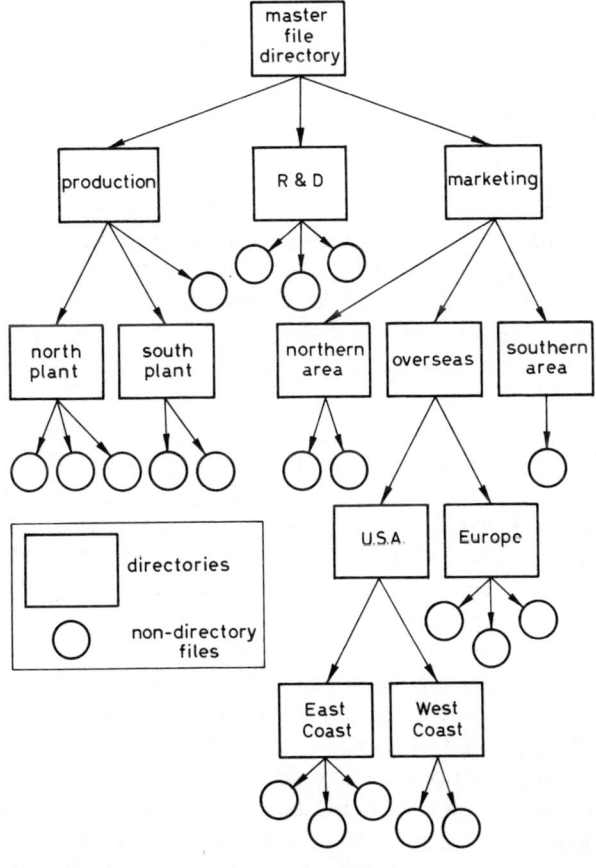

Fig. 2.1

In designing a filing system, it is natural to think in terms of a hierarchical structure. In such a structure some or all of the entries in the higher level directories will be other directories. Only at the lower levels will the directories consist of entries which are entirely non-directory files. A typical filing system is shown in Fig. 2.1. A hierarchical system caters for the needs of users who are organized into groups and sub-groups; it may also be used to reflect the structure of an organization for administrative and accounting purposes. One advantage of a time-sharing system is the ease with which users may share information. An example of such a need is when a group of programmers is working on a number of programs which share a common data base. It is necessary, therefore, that provision be made in a filing system for a user to obtain access to files belonging to another user. This may be achieved by allowing users to set up links directly to another user's files, or by allowing reference to files prefixed by a user name. It should be noted that there may be a multiplicity of files within the filing system with the same name, but within a user's directory each file must have a unique name. User names are, of course, unique to avoid any ambiguity at login time.

The information kept in the filing system by a user must be accessible by that user only, unless that user takes specific steps to share the file. The protection provided by systems varies enormously. Some simple systems give no protection other than the user name, others give one or more of the following protection schemes.

The outermost protection is given at login time when the identity of the user is being established. Each user has a unique user name which generally is displayed at the terminal at login. Thus, anyone anxious to break the security of the system has merely to look over our shoulder. Equally, a user who has a user name, differing from our own by a single character may by accident login under the wrong name and if no further check is applied gain access to our files and charge his use of the system to our account. A simple security device at this stage is for the system to demand a password as well as a user name. The password may be masked either by overprinting it or by inhibiting the printing at the terminal.

Other checks which may be applied are concerned with the identity of the terminal at which we are sitting. With an in-house system, where all of the terminals are permanently connected to the system (as opposed to those which use the telephone system to make a temporary connection), the unique line to which the terminal is attached may be identified by the system and a check may be made to ensure that we have permission to login at this terminal. Thus, for example, only the managing director may login on the terminal in the managing director's office! With a dial-up system (i.e., a system using the telephone system to make connections between the terminals and the computer) it is usually possible to identify each terminal if this is required. For example, on a teletype we may install a device called an 'answer-back drum'. Such a device, when fitted to a teletype, causes a group of characters to be transmitted to the computer on receipt of a signal from the computer. The particular group of characters sent may be determined when the drum is fitted to the teletype. Thus, by making the group of characters different on each of the terminals on the system it is possible to identify the terminal automatically. Another useful security device is to restrict access to the machine to certain times only for specific persons.

The inner level of protection is concerned with individual files within a user's directory. Once again, a password can be demanded as well as the name of the file. When listing out the names of files held within the directory, the passwords must not of course be printed, only the file names.

As we have stated earlier, it is necessary to enable users to share files with other users. One way to achieve this is to allow entries in our directory relating to files owned by another user, with that user's permission and cooperation. There would, of course, be a command to accomplish this. The owner of the file would have to add our user name to the list of users who may access the file in question, using commands provided for the purpose. The advantage of setting up such links is that linked files become as easy to use as our own files. An alternative arrangement is for us to refer to the file, not just by a single name but by a name compounded of the owner's name followed by the file name, e.g., BILL: PROGX. Once again, such an access would only be allowed if the owner (BILL) had appended our user name to the list of those users able to access file PROGX.

A refinement often provided with file sharing is to give the owner the ability to classify the mode or modes of access he is willing to permit on a given file. In this way, the owner is able to restrict the capabilities which a user has when accessing the file. Typically, the modes of access are read, write, execute, append, and change status. If file sharing is accomplished by allowing users to set up links, then a further mode of access may be provided saying whether or not the user may permit access to the link by other users. The meaning of the various modes of access depends upon the type of file to which it is applied.

If the file is a non-directory file, read allows the file to be listed; write allows the directory; write allows a user to change the contents of the directory, which includes the adding of new files, and the deleting and the changing of names of existing files within the directory; execute allows the user to search the directory (i.e., to see if a particular file exists within the directory); append allows new files (entries in the directory) to be added; and change status allows a user to append and delete user names from the access lists of files within the directory, and to change the modes of access allowed to any user on any file within the directory.

If the file is a non-directory file, real allows the file to be listed; write allows the contents of the file to be changed; execute allows the file to be executed as a program or as part of a program; append allows data to be added to the end of the file only (i.e., it is more restrictive than write); and change status allows the user to change the status of the file.

When a user attempts to access a file, a check is made to ensure (a) that the user's name appears in the list of users allowed to access the file and (b) that the

27

capability required by this user is permitted according to the modes set against his name in the list. Although the control of capabilities is primarily provided to protect the owner's files from other users, similar checks are usually applied to the owner also. To cover this situation, there is a free mode which gives a user all the capabilities possible, and this is automatically given to the owner of a file when the file first comes into being. However, there are situations where the owner of a file may wish to limit his own access capabilities. For example, if a file is of particular value, it may pay an owner to give himself only the capability to read and the power to change status (it is not usually possible for an owner to take the power to change status away from himself), thereby avoiding the possibility of overwriting or discarding the file accidentally. If the file needs updating he can temporarily change his own status to accomplish this.

There are a number of variants on the above scheme. One simpler scheme is to provide two ways of accessing a file—with and without password rather than having a list of permitted users. Those who know the password of the file may get one set of capabilities, those users who only know the file name will receive more limited capabilities.

In the foregoing, we have discussed file protection against such things as illegal users, accidental or malicious damage by users permitted access to files, self-inflicted accidents, and accidental or malicious damage by users denied access to files.

The problems of providing protection against hardware and filing system software failures are discussed in section 5.3.

It is clear that if users are allowed to retain as much information as they wish within the filing system, the faster devices such as drums and discs may well become full. In this case some files may have to be moved to slower devices such as magnetic tape. The files held on magnetic tape should not be those currently in frequent use by users. Thus, little-used files will be relegated to slow-access devices and may even find their way off-line to dismounted reels of magnetic tape. If a file not held on-line is called for by a user, a message is sent to the operator telling him to mount the appropriate tape and from there it is copied to a faster device. Often, in such a situation, a courtesy message would be sent to the user to inform him of the delay involved in the operation. As files are moved within the backing store, based on the usage of the file, the position of the file is recorded within the directory. If the file ends up on a dismounted magnetic tape, the tape name will be kept in the directory so that the appropriate information can be sent to the operator to enable him to identify the required tape.

2.4 Editors

Line editors. On-line source file editing is fundamental to time-sharing and all systems provide editing facilities. The more powerful the editor, the more useful it is to the experienced user. We may classify editors into three categories—those providing only the basic essentials of deleting, inserting, adding, and replacing lines; more sophisticated line editors; and text editors.

An example of the first type of editing is provided in our earlier example of AID (JOSS). Here, the user supplies a step number and the step number serves to order the lines of the program. A line may be inserted between two other lines by selecting an intermediate step number. A line is added to the end of a program by selecting a step number higher than any previous step numbers. A line may be replaced by retyping with the same step number. A line may be deleted by typing DELETE, followed by the step number. In other systems, there may be a slightly different technique for deleting the line but the facilities remain the same. On some systems, the line numbers are supplied by the system rather than by the user, so that before deleting, inserting, or replacing a line (other than perhaps the last line typed), the line number must be reset to the appropriate value by an editing command. In all other respects, the facilities will be very much the same as those on a system where the user supplies the line numbers. A simple example of the above facilities is given below in BASIC. In this language, the user supplies the line numbers. To delete a line, we type the line number followed immediately by a carriage return. The program, incidentally, calculates the sum and the sum of the squares of a set of numbers.

SYSTEM--BASIC	tell the system we are going to use BASIC
NEW OR OLD--NEW	create a new file
NEW FILE NAME--EDITEX	call it EDITEX
READY.	
10 READ N	
20 FOR I=1 TO N	
30 READ X	
40 LET Y=X↑2	
50 LET S=S+X	
60 LET S=S+Y	
70 NEXT I	
80 PRINT S	
90 DATA 6,1,2,3,4,5,6	
100 END	
15 LET S=S2=0	insert line 15
60 LET S2=S2+X↑2	replace line 60
40	delete line 40
80 PRINT S,S2	replace line 80
90 DATA 6	replace line 90
95 DATA 1,2,3,4,5,6	insert line 95
85 GOTO 10	insert line 85
80 PRINT "SUM=";S;"SUM OF SQUARES=";S2	replace (again) line 80
LIST	ask for a listing of the program as it now stands

EDITEX 14:17

10 READ N

```
15 LET S=S2=0
20 FOR I=1 TO N                     note: insertions appear in their
30 READ X                           correct place, line 40 has
50 LET S=S+X                        disappeared and that the
60 LET S2=S2+X↑2                    last versions of lines 60, 80
70 NEXT I                           and 90 are the ones that occur
80 PRINT "SUM=";S;"SUM OF SQUARES=";S2
85 GOTO 10
90 DATA 6
95 DATA 1,2,3,4,5,6
100 END

RUN                                 run the program

EDITEX 14:18

SUM= 21    SUM OF SQUARES= 91       results

OUT OF DATA IN 10                   exit from program


USED     2.17 SEC.                  2.17 seconds of central processor time used
```

The more sophisticated line editors are still concerned with the line as the basic unit of information, but provide many other useful functions over and above the basic essentials. An example of a line editor is that provided in the Dartmouth College (Hanover, N.H., U.S.A.) Time-Sharing System (DTSS). The editor is called into action by typing EDIT, followed by one or more commands to the editor. The descriptions below are taken from Dartmouth Technical Memorandum TM 002. In some cases, for the sake of simplicity, the description is not quite as in the manual, and in a number of cases certain features of the command have been omitted.

The term 'current file', in the descriptions below, refers to the file most recently fetched by the user from the filing system. Those commands which have a list of file names as parameters work on files held in the filing system rather than the user's current file, but return the results of the edit to the user's current file. When operating on the current file, the copy of this file held in the filing system is unchanged, all changes being made to the copy opened by the user. It is worth noting, in passing, that it is possible for more than one user to have an open copy of the same file independently of one another.

APPEND followed by a list of file names: the individual files in the list are concatenated into a single file, which is then resequenced (see RESEQUENCE).
JOIN list of files: the files are combined into a single file but not resequenced.
MERGE list of file names: the files are combined according to line numbers. No line numbers are changed. If two or more files have lines with the same number, the line which will appear will be the one from the last file in the list in which that line appeared.

DELETE L1, L2, L3, ... : where L is either a single line number or a pair of line numbers separated by a hyphen indicating a group of lines. The command will remove the lines or groups of lines from the user's current file.

EXTRACT L1, L2, L3, ... : this command (the opposite of DELETE) preserves the lines or groups of lines specified from the user's current file, discarding all other lines.

MOVE L1, L2: L1 is either a single line number or a group of lines. L2 is a single line number. MOVE takes the line or lines specified by L1 and places them after line L2.

DESEQUENCE: removes all line numbers from the user's current file.

RESEQUENCE: this is one of the most powerful editing functions and allows us to put a new set of line numbers on our current file in a variety of ways.

SEQUENCE: this command places an entirely new set of line numbers on the user's current file.

LIST: types single lines, groups of lines, or the entire current file either forwards or in reverse order.

LOCATE 'string': searches the user's current file for any occurrence of the specified string and prints out on the terminal all lines which contain a reference to the string. (A string is just a sequence of characters.)

PAGE list of file names: lists the files in the order listed on notebook-size pages. Each page begins with a page number and the name of the file currently being listed. A new page is started for each file.

EXPLAIN followed by the name of an edit function: this most valuable command types out a short description of the specified edit function giving command format, description of how it works, and one or more examples of its use.

Text editors. Text editors operate on characters or groups of characters rather than lines as their basic unit of information. Once again, an excellent editor of this type is to be found on DTSS, and a very brief description, taken from the same source as the line editor—this time, Technical Memorandum TM 003,—is given below. Before embarking on a description of the commands available, a few comments are in order. Text is always scanned from left to right along a line and from top to bottom of the lines in the file. The scanning is aided by two pointers, called 'left and right string pointers'. They are used to mark positions in the search file. The string of characters enclosed by the pointers is known as the 'current string'. The editor operates by scanning for strings in the search file (the user's current file) and copying portions of this file into an output (results) file, depending upon the commands given. Thus the editor does not make changes 'in place' but carries out the work in the output file.

There are over thirty edit commands available and these may be grouped according to their action. Not all the available commands are described and the description has been simplified in a number of cases.

Commands which manipulate the string pointers

BOTTOM: the two pointers are moved to point to the null (empty) string at the end of the current file.
TOP: similar to BOTTOM, only the pointers are moved to the beginning of the file.
LEFT: the right pointer is moved to coincide with the left pointer.
RIGHT: the left pointer is moved to coincide with the right pointer.
SAVE name: the position of the two pointers is saved under the name specified.
RESTORE name: the two pointers are reset to the position they had when last SAVEd under the specified name.

Commands to define expressions
SET #n, string: defines the string specified to be numbered for later reference by other commands as string n.

Commands used to search for and to copy text to the output file
COPY: current string is copied to the output file.
OUTPUT string: the specified string is copied to the output file.
FIND n, m: search for the mth occurence of string n copying to the output file all text up to but not including the mth occurence. The pointers are set around the mth occurence of string n. There are five other commands, SKIP, DELETE, REPLACE, INSERT, and PREFIX which are variants of FIND in that they find the mth occurence of string n and skip all text on the way, delete all occurrences of the string on the way, replace all occurrences of string n by a specified string, and insert a specified string before and after each occurence of string n.

Commands to control the result of the edit
EXIT: the search file is copied to the output file from the right pointer to the end of the file. The output file becomes the user's current file and the edit is terminated.
STOP: the edit is terminated and all changes are lost, the user's current file is as it was before the edit.

Commands to inform the user of the current state of the edit
PRINT: the current string is printed on the terminal.
LOCATE n, m: lines containing all or part of the string n are printed up to the mth occurrence of string n.
EXPLAIN command name: an explanation of the named command is typed on the terminal as in the line editor.

Files of commands. It is possible to write an editing program and store this program in a file. The program is then called into action by the command FILE followed by the name of the file. All the editing commands described above may be included in an editing file but a number of extra commands available only for use in files are provided. A simple example is given below to illustrate some of the extra facilities.

Suppose we wish to change every other occurrence of MONDAY to TUESDAY in our current file (an unlikely event, but it will serve as an example). If we had previously created the file X containing the following:

100 SET 3, MONDAY	set string 3 to MONDAY
110 FIND 3,1	find 1st occurrence of MONDAY
120 IF EOF THEN 160	if end of file reached, stop
130 COPY	copy MONDAY
140 REPLACE, 3, TUESDAY, 1	replace next MONDAY by TUESDAY
150 IF MORE THEN 110	if not at end of file, go back or
160 EXIT	exit from edit.

then we may accomplish this edit by typing
EDIT FILE X

The two editors cited above are given in some detail so that they may be used as a guide in evaluating the editing capabilities of a given system. Few systems will provide the range of facilities offered by the DTSS editors, although hopefully this situation will change with time.

The importance of a good range of editing facilities ranging from the simple for the casual user of the system to the more powerful for the experienced users cannot be over-emphasized. In the debugging of a program, it is essential that the corrections to the source program can be made as quickly and conveniently as possible.

Finally, when dealing with large data bases in a time-sharing environment, it is essential that a sophisticated editor is available for data base maintenance. For example, suppose as part of the data base there exists a list of items by part numbers. If it is required to change the part number of an item, it is essential that all references to this item within other items be updated. It is clear that a text editor is capable of doing this very simply and with little risk of error.

2.5 Debugging Aids

The basic requirements for debugging are good source-editing facilities, better than average compile-time and run-time diagnostic messages, and some run-time fault-finding aids. We have discussed the importance of editors in the last section, but it is worth spending some time on specific examples which arise in debugging situations. Suppose we wish to change the name of a variable everywhere it occurs in a program. This situation may arise in, say, BASIC when calling another program as a subprogram and a clash of names occurs. To accomplish the name change, we may scan a listing of the program by eye and retype each line in which the name occurs—a very tedious and error prone technique. Alternatively, we may use a text editor and accomplish this in one or two commands. Frequently, in debugging, we find that in order to correct the logic of a program we must insert a number of lines of program. If commands such as INSERT and RESEQUENCE are not available, we must renumber the lines ourselves if insufficient space exists between the lines for the insert. In such languages as BASIC, where the line numbers also serve as labels, such renumbering is error-prone, since we may omit to change references elsewhere to the renumbered lines. The edit command RESEQUENCE on DTSS will, in the case of BASIC, change not only the line numbers but also references to them within the program.

It is obvious that if time is not to be wasted sitting at the terminal poring over manuals to discover the meaning of an error message, it is necessary that error messages given by the compiler and by the program when it fails at run-time, should be as informative as possible. In the case of compiler messages, it should be possible to isolate the cause of the error in the source program in all cases directly from the error message.

Run-time error messages should inform the user of the position within the source program where the error has been detected. This will generally be accompanied by indicating a line number. The message should also give as much information as possible regarding the variables associated with the error, together with their values. The type of run-time error should be identified by the message without causing the user to refer to the manual to clarify obscure points.

We may classify run-time debugging aids into two classes—static and dynamic. Static debugging aids enable us to examine what is going on as a program runs and/or the state of the program when it has stopped running. In either case, we are not able to control the action of the program. Dynamic debugging techniques, on the other hand, allow us to do all of the static tests as well as allowing us to control the program as it runs, making changes to the program and making decisions dynamically about our next move. Static aids are easier to provide and make less demands upon the system. If all the work on the system is to be carried out in a high-level programming language such as FORTRAN then good static aids may well prove to be adequate. Dynamic aids are more demanding upon the system but in most cases this overhead is more than compensated for by the speed with which programs can be developed. This is particularly true in the case of assembly language programming.

The number and quality of static facilities provided vary from system to system. The static aids we might look for in a good system, some of which we would apply to monitor a program run and some after the run as a post-mortem, are as follows. Before running a program, we should like to arrange for the name and value of variables to be printed at the terminal whenever their value changes during execution, and for the printing of a trace of each control transfer that takes place during execution, particularly on such transfers as subprogram linkage. It is also useful to be able to set up one or more break-points which stop execution at particular statements, thus isolating parts of the program. After the program has stopped, we should like to be able to look at the value of all or selected variables in the program and to obtain a listing of all statements which were not obeyed and all variables which were not referenced. It is also useful to be able to obtain a cross-reference listing, telling us which statements in the program make reference to each individual variable, label, and constant.

Dynamic debugging techniques give us control over the execution of the program and allow us to modify the program and monitor its progress. In particular, we are able to accomplish some or all of the following:

(a) Interrupt a running program and gain control. The system should respond to an interruption by indicating the statement about to be executed.

(b) Print the values of selected variables.

(c) Change the program by submitting new statements in the source language without causing a recompilation of the entire program and without changing the rest of the program (except where such change is implied by the introduction of the new statement).

(d) Change the value of selected variables.

(e) Cause one or more statements of the program to be executed.

(f) Set or unset break points within the program.

(g) Set or unset a trace on the flow of control within various regions of the program.

(h) Continue after an interruption or on meeting a break point, or transfer control to any statement within the program.

Apart from interrupting a running program, all other facilities may be used before, after, or during a run. With such facilities, it is possible to locate and correct errors in a fraction of the time required without them. It is essential that dynamic debugging allows the user to work in the source language when making changes to the program rather than in some lower-level language. It is also useful to have available the means of comparing two programs and printing the differences between them. In this way, changes made during a debugging or editing session may be identified.

A special mention should be made of JOSS-type languages, in that their design is such that dynamic debugging techniques are built into the language. We will use TELCOMP to give an example of dynamic debugging. Suppose we wish to write a program to sort n numbers into descending order, the following dialog might take place.

±1.1 DEMAND N	To sort N numbers into descending order
±1.3 DO PART 2 FOR I=1:1:N	Part 2 demands N numbers
±1.4 DO PART 3 FOR I=1:1:N	Part 3 does the sorting
±1.5 DO PART 5 FOR I=1:1:N	Part 5 prints the results
±1.6 STOP	
±2.1 DEMAND A[I]	
±3.1 DONE IF A[I]▷A[I+1]	If A[I]▷ A[I+1] these two numbers are in order
±3.2 DO PART 4 FOR J=I:-1:1	If not move A[I+1] into its correct place
±4.1 DONE IF A[J]<A[J+1]	Stop when it gets there

±4.2 SET A[J]=A[J+1]	Exchange A[J] and A[J+1]
±4.3 SET A[J+1]=A[J]	
±5.1 TYPE A[I]	
±DO PART 1	Execute the program
N=10	There are to be 10 numbers
A[1]=9	
A[2]=8	
A[3]=7	
A[4]=4	
A[5]=5	These are the 10 numbers to be sorted
A[6]=6	
A[7]=1	
A[8]=9	
A[9]=3	
A[10]=2	
ERROR AT STEP 3.1	At step 3.1 we have tried to access A[11]
A[11] IS UNDEFINED	We must look at the value of I
±TYPE I	
I= 10	with I=10, I+1=11, hence the error
±1.4 DO PART 3 FOR I=1:1:N-1	correct the end of range value of I
±DO STEP 1.4	Using the current values of A[1]-A[10] sort again
±DO STEP 1.5	and print the results
A[1]= 1	
A[2]= 1	
A[3]= 1	
A[4]= 1	
A[5]= 1	
A[6]= 1	
A[7]= 1	
A[8]= 9	
A[9]= 3	
A[10]= 2	Values have been corrupted
±4.4 TYPE A[J],A[J+1],J,I	Arrange for intermediate values to be printed
±DO PART 1	Start again since the values have been spoilt
N=10	
A[1]=9	
A[2]=8	
A[3]=7	
A[4]=4	
A[5]=5	
A[6]=6	
A[7]=1	
A[8]=9	
A[9]=3	
A[10]=2	
A[3]= 4	The first exchange is between A[3] and A[4]; it should be between A[4] and A[5]. Not only this, but we have lost the value of A[3]
A[4]= 4	
J= 3	
I= 4	

	A[2]=	4	Then we lose the value of A[2]
	A[3]=	4	
	J=	2	
	I=	4	
	A[1]=	4	Everything is being set to 4! This points
	A[2]=	4	to the exchange routine. On looking, we
	J=	1	see that in step 4.2 we discard the
	I=	4	value of A[J] when we need it for later.
	A[3]=	4	We must take steps to preserve it.
	A[4]=	4	
	J=	3	
	I=	5	

INTERRUPTED AT STEP 4.4   Interrupt the program by striking the
                                           break key
±4.2 SET T=A[J]   Do the exchange properly
±4.3 SET A[J]=A[J+1]
±4.4 SET A[J+1]=T   This deletes the type statement inserted
                                           earlier
±DO PART 1   Start again to get new data

	N=10		
	A[1]=9		
	A[2]=8		
	A[3]=7		
	A[4]=4		
	A[5]=5		
	A[6]=6		
	A[7]=1		
	A[8]=9		
	A[9]=3		
	A[10]=2		
	A[1]=	1	We seem to have cured one problem but
	A[2]=	4	not all. There are signs in the first four
	A[3]=	5	that we are sorting into ascending order.
	A[4]=	9	Check the comparisons in steps 3.1 and
	A[5]=	8	4.1
	A[6]=	7	
	A[7]=	6	Step 4.1 is the troublemaker
	A[8]=	9	
	A[9]=	3	
	A[10]=	2	

STOPPED AT STEP   1.6   Interrupt the program
±4.1 DONE IF A[J] > A[J+1]   Correct step 4.1
±DO STEP 1.4   Sort again
±DO STEP 1.5   Print results

	A[1]=	9	
	A[2]=	9	
	A[3]=	8	
	A[4]=	7	
	A[5]=	6	
	A[6]=	5	
	A[7]=	4	
	A[8]=	3	
	A[9]=	2	
	A[10]=	1	Correct!

```
⇇TYPE ALL PARTS            List the program as it now stands.
 ┌ 1.1 DEMAND N
   1.3 DO PART 2 FOR I=1:1:N
   1.4 DO PART 3 FOR I=1:1:N-1
   1.5 DO PART 5 FOR I=1:1:N
   1.6 STOP

   2.1 DEMAND A[I]
   3.1 DONE IF A[I] > A[I+1]
   3.2 DO PART 4 FOR J=I:-1:1
   4.1 DONE IF A[J] > A[J+1]
   4.2 SET T=A[J]
   4.3 SET A[J]=A[J+1]
   4.4 SET A[J+1]=T
   5.1 TYPE A[I]
 └    ←
```

2.6 Terminal Devices

We do not intend to review the immense number and variety of terminal devices available currently, for to do so would make this section no more than a list of manufacturers' brochures. However, it is useful to classify terminal devices into broad categories in order to distinguish typical characteristics.

Typewriter-like devices. The most common of this class of device is the Teletype—the brand name of a particular teleprinter. The Teletype, because of its price, its characteristics, and its availability at the right time, is currently the most common of all time-sharing terminals. Typically, devices in this class have a keyboard and a printer and may have associated paper tape input and output. Such devices are relatively cheap and it is this that makes them attractive propositions. They have an operating speed of between ten and twenty characters per second, which is more than adequate for human input but at times a little slow for output, particularly for anything other than a few lines. A recent addition to terminals of this type has been a plotter interface, allowing an incremental plotter to be attached, giving slow, hard copy graphic facilities. The cost of the plotter far outweighs the cost of the rest of the terminal.

Character displays. A character display may be regarded as a typewriter-like device with the printer replaced by a video display. This offers a number of advantages. The devices are virtually silent, and the output of characters is very much faster than on an electromechanical device. Since the terminal is essentially electronic rather than electromechanical, it is more reliable than a typewriter-like device. Many character displays offer local editing facilities. When characters are entered from the keyboard they are displayed on the screen and held in a buffer within the terminal. The contents of this buffer, and hence the display, may be changed with the aid of a moving pointer and a number of special keys. Only when the operator is satisfied with the contents of the buffer is the information transmitted to the central computer.

A hard copy may be obtained by attaching an electromechanical printing mechanism to the display, but if frequent use is made of this, many of the advantages of the display are lost. The cost of a simple display is roughly that of a heavy-duty typewriter-like device, but rather more if a hard copy printer is added. This type of terminal is coming down in price and is likely to be in widespread use in the very near future.

Graphic displays. For many applications, alpha-numeric data is not sufficient. For example, for engineering and other design applications, graphs and diagrams are normal communication forms. Diagrams may be easily produced on a line-drawing cathode ray tube or on some sort of plotting device, but it is desirable that the diagram be manipulated dynamically at run-time as a result of user commands issued at the terminal. The user needs to be able to add new elements, delete elements or modify the size and position of the diagram.

The hardware for displaying graphical output can be divided into two categories—static and interactive devices. Static devices are those where the elements within the image cannot be changed by user commands without regeneration of the entire image. Interactive devices are those which display an image for a relatively short time, and therefore have to be refreshed repeatedly in order to maintain a continuous image. The refresh rate must be of the order of 30–40 times per second in order that the human eye registers a 'flicker-free' picture.

One type of interactive graphics terminal consists of a cathode ray tube and a light pen (a photo-cell on the end of a 'pen-like' rod). A spot of light controlled by the computer is moved across the screen. If the light-pen is placed against the screen, then as the spot passes beneath the photocell, a pulse is emitted and used to record the current position of the pen. The position of the pen may be constantly monitored and its path traced, thus facilitating the drawing of diagrams. One may also use the pen to point to that part of the current display about which an instruction is to be given via the terminal.

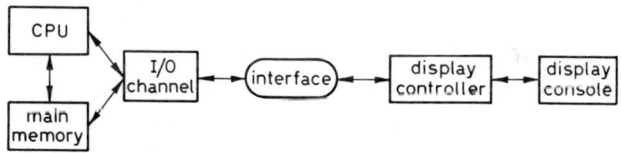

Fig. 2.2

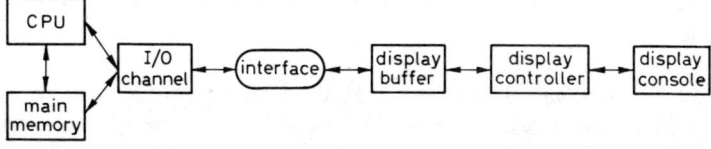

Fig. 2.3

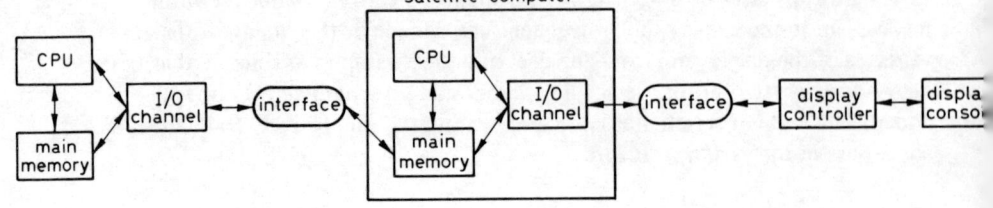

Fig. 2.4

In interfacing a graphics display to a computer, it is necessary to provide control logic to decode display commands prepared by the computer and to drive the display console. The need to refresh 30–40 times per second is a significant factor in interface design. Figures 2.2, 2.3, and 2.4 illustrate computer–display interfaces. In Fig. 2.2, the computer provides the necessary refresh. However, one problem posed by interfacing a graphics system to a time-sharing system is that each user on the time-sharing system is serviced at intervals. It is clear that in the case of the light-pen, for example, if it is to be followed across the screen the display must be serviced continuously. In Fig. 2.3, a separate refresh memory, the display buffer, together with the display controller, provides the refresh. In Fig. 2.4, a small digital computer is used both as the display buffer and for display housekeeping. This latter method of interfacing overcomes the problem of tracing a light-pen in a time-sharing environment.

A brief mention should be made of the developing use of graphic techniques in large-scale experimental work. For example, major steps are being taken in the field of X-ray crystallography, where programs are now available that will display a molecular structure (from the electron density data), allow it to be turned through any angle, and also enable cross-sections to be viewed. It is a relatively small step before the use of a time-sharing system will enable data to be transmitted to the main system, be processed and then transmitted back for viewing directly at an experimental site. Similar lines are being followed in the area of analysis of particle-track photographs in high-energy physics, although the problems of pattern recognition are severe. It is therefore not unreasonable to visualize the the significance, in a variety of large experimental areas, of large-scale time-sharing systems in conjunction with graphical display techniques, enabling man to interact with a system, using his intuition to guide the solution to massive problems. In this way, optimum solutions may be produced in a relatively short period of time, which with traditional batch-processing methods may never be reached.

Remote batch terminals. This type of terminal differs from the previous ones in that it is not designed as an interactive terminal. However, many time-sharing systems have such terminals attached. A simple remote batch terminal may consist of a card reader and a slow line printer. Alternatively, it may be a sophisticated system with a small satellite computer with a range of peripherals such as a card reader, paper tape reader, line printer, and magnetic tape units. Given such a satellite computer, it may be possible and desirable to use it to handle a large number of simple time-sharing terminals local to the satellite, thus saving telephone charges, since only one line from the satellite computer to the main system would be used rather than one line for each terminal if no satellite computer was available. A large number of time-sharing bureaux are using or about to use this principle of a satellite computer, acting as a 'concentrator', in order to reduce line changes for those users who are long distances from the time-sharing centre. The users are connected to a local system (the concentrator) which is then connected, via a high-speed line, to the main system.

In conclusion, it is likely that as far as general problem-solving time-sharing is concerned the Teletype and the simple character display are with us for some time yet. The graphics terminal will increasingly be used in the field of computer-aided design, and a number will be attached to in-house time-sharing systems. The remote batch terminal will be used where high-volume data processing is required from a remote site and as time-sharing software is easily adapted to deal with such terminals it is likely that they will appear on an increasingly large number of time-sharing systems.

3 Methods of Achieving Time-Sharing

> To do two things at once is to do neither.
> Pubilius Syrus

3.1 Introduction

Although the following chapter is subdivided into sections which highlight the major methods of achieving time-sharing, it must be noted that with the large number and variety of computers now available many will exhibit characteristics belonging to more than one section. In general, we can say that one of the following methods will be adopted as a basis for time-sharing on a given system. However, note that after changing the configuration slightly one may well find that on a given system another technique is more applicable. This particular point cannot be over-emphasized, since if we are evaluating a time-sharing system this evaluation must take into account not only the capabilities of the current system, but also how those capabilities may change if and when the system is expanded. Any expansion, say, in terms of available main memory or enhanced peripheral devices, may place the system in a different category providing more powerful facilities.

3.2 Remote Job Entry

In order to appreciate the simplest approach to achieving a limited form of time-sharing (under our definition) let us consider a simple batch-processing system capable of accepting jobs and associated commands, say from a card reader, and filing them on some suitable backing storage (i.e., disc) for subsequent processing. We therefore have a queue of jobs from which the next job to be processed is selected, loaded into main memory and then run until complete. When a particular job is finished, the next in sequence is selected from the queue, loaded, and run. Thus, we have a system which is running one user program at a time (uniprogramming) and selecting the next job to be run from the job queue. (Note that we shall use the terms 'uniprogramming' and 'multiprogramming' applied to one or many *user* programs. For example, in an environment where only a single user program can be run, other events will be taking place within the operating system simultaneously; in spite of this, we shall still term this 'uniprogramming'.)

To obtain a time-sharing environment, it is necessary for this system to allow, firstly, jobs to be entered into the job queue by terminal users in exactly the same manner as jobs entered say, at the card reader and, secondly, give to the terminal user some interactive capability.

As we have seen earlier, quite a large number of tasks undertaken by the terminal user make relatively trivial demands on the computer's available processing time. For example, if we are creating a program at the terminal we require the means to file each line of the source program as it is created on backing store, plus the ability to delete or replace any lines we may have created in error. In this relatively simple approach to time-sharing, it is not until our program (job) file is complete that we need to ask the computer to compile and perhaps execute our program. It is at this stage, when we give a command from the terminal to run our particular job, that it is entered into the normal job queue for processing. This mode of operation is generally called 'remote job entry'. The method by which this form of time-sharing is achieved is as follows.

To the computer's supervisor routines and operating system is added specific remote job entry software, which when loaded is responsible for processing commands submitted at the user terminals. Thus, this software communicates with the terminals while the standard operating system processes batch jobs normally. Once a terminal is linked to this remote job entry software, it will enable the user by means of simple commands to perform various operations such as: create a file, delete a file, access a previously stored file, edit an existing file, list a file (i.e., to obtain results and check editing) and submit a job to the standard operating system for, say, compilation and execution. It is when the user gives the command for submission of the job to the batch-processing system that his job then enters the queue and will subsequently be processed along with other terminal and normal batch jobs. Figure 3.1 indicates the general arrangement of data in the computer.

We can see that in a uniprogramming system (running only one user at a time), where all jobs are run to completion, once a terminal user has submitted his job to the batch queue he will have to wait an indeterminate amount of time before results are transmitted, via the remote job entry software, back to his terminal. For example, there may be a large batch job preceding a particular terminal job in the job queue, which would involve very large delays before the terminal job were processed. It is therefore impractical to return results of terminal jobs directly to the user terminal with such large possible delays involved. Terminals would be inactive for long periods of time while results were awaited,

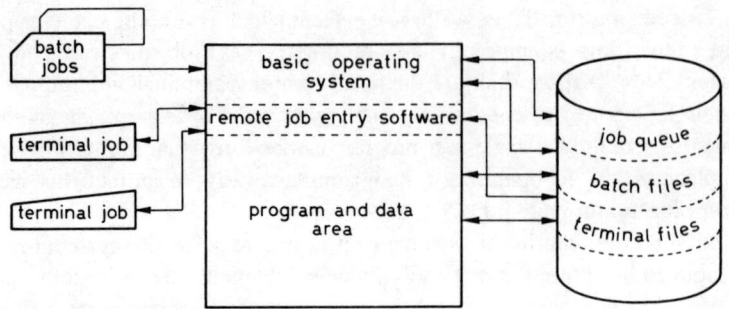

Fig. 3.1 A simple representation of a possible main memory layout, file structure, and data flow within a remote job entry system

during which time other users or other jobs could be set up from the terminal. Therefore, the normal procedure for remote job entry systems is to have an output file area on the backing storage to which results are returned (i.e., compiled program and error diagnostics). Each user can then interrogate from the terminal his particular output file at some later time.

With a system of the above type, where the aim is high machine utilization with restricted time-sharing capabilities, we should expect multiprogramming ability. That is, the computer should be able to hold in main memory a number of user programs simultaneously, running these programs at intervals. So that, for example, when a program reaches a temporarily inactive state, such as waiting for a transfer of data from a peripheral, another of the programs can be activated, thereby utilizing what would effectively be idle time if there were only one program in main memory. Unfortunately, even with this increased machine performance as a result of multiprogramming, we are still not in a position to transfer results directly to a terminal and guarantee a reasonable response time. Therefore, this type of system will still maintain the principle of an output results file available for subsequent interrogation. It is important to note that any system capable of multiprogramming will generally need to maintain input and output files on backing store. In a batch-processing system it is quite likely that, for example, two programs being processed simultaneously require output to the line printer (assuming only one line printer on the system). Therefore it is necessary for at least one of these programs to store its results temporarily on backing storage until the line printer is free (i.e., spooling).

Finally, to make the system completely viable, it is necessary to maintain some form of priority structure for those jobs, whether batch- or terminal-generated, in the current job queue. A simple sequential queue where jobs are run on a first-in, first-out basis would be totally inadequate for normal operational purposes. A common solution to this problem is to allow the user and/or the operating system to supply a numeric or alphanumeric code to a given job in order to classify that job. When the job queue is scanned by the operating system, the job classification will determine which job is to be run next.

Obviously, under operational conditions it is important to allow jobs of some urgency to be run before less urgent tasks. Aside from a simple, priority-coded scheduling algorithm many other considerations have to be taken into account in designing the particular scheduling algorithm. For example, a low-priority job may be passed over for processing many times if jobs currently in the queue and jobs entering the queue have higher priority. Therefore, a number of computer systems incorporate within the job description a count of how many times a job is passed over. When a job is passed over a set number of times (the number of times can usually be varied by an installation controlled parameter) the job will then automatically be run. The design of scheduling algorithms is dealt with in section 5.2. However, the ability of a particular computer system to schedule work effectively is one that must not be overlooked or underestimated when evaluating the system.

As we shall emphasize a number of times throughout this book, whether a given system offers distinct advantages or disadvantages when compared with other systems depends to a large extent on the type of use to which a prospective user is going to put the system. Therefore, although we shall now highlight briefly what we consider to be the advantages or disadvantages of remote job entry, they should be viewed in the light of individual requirements.

Advantages

(a) In terms of time-sharing demands, the system is not being subjected to the need for giving fast response to a terminal for those tasks which are particularly time-consuming (i.e., compilation and execution). The system is only giving direct terminal response to the less demanding tasks, such as file building.

(b) The command language can be simplified, since the terminal user is only interacting with the system at the file creation and editing stage and not at the stage where he can exercise control over the running program. This makes the use of a terminal considerably more straightforward for the uninitiated.

(c) The fact that all jobs, whether batch or terminal generated, are run to completion means that the machine utilization (i.e., making the best use of the computer's processing capability) is very good. This assumes, of course, that the computer under consideration has effective multiprogramming ability.

(d) The terminal user, once he has submitted a job for processing, is operating with exactly the same facilities as a batch user. This means he has all the available software, which can of course be vast, at his disposal. This is not necessarily true of other methods of achieving time-sharing. The terminal user often has only a specific, restricted version of the system's total available software within which to operate.

(e) It is often possible for a remote job entry system to support more simultaneous terminal users than some of the other systems employing different techniques. This is simply because the user is placing fewer demands on the computing system and is likewise receiving less comprehensive facilities.

(f) The design philosophy (i.e., running terminal jobs under a batch-operating

system) is ideally suited to inputting and outputting large programs and/or large volumes of data to or from remote terminals. In order to sustain this type of operation, it should be obvious that the remote terminal must be capable of achieving adequate input or output speeds. This mode of operation, large remote job processing via fast terminal devices (i.e., card readers, line printers, other computers, etc.), will not be considered further, as it does not qualify as true time-sharing under our definition. It is included as an advantage since it is a growing area of particular importance in the sphere of data processing.

Disadvantage
Within the context of this book, the disadvantage of remote job entry can be summarized briefly. It does not offer a true time-sharing system. The terminal user does not have the ability to interact with his job once it has been submitted for processing. He does not have the facilities available to fully develop a program whilst continuously on-line to the system. Remote job entry is a compromise between the two concepts of a standard batch-processing system and a time-sharing system.

3.3 Roll-in/Roll-out Job Streams

In order to achieve a true time-sharing situation, where a number of terminal users are interacting with their program at various stages in its development, two general principles are fundamental.

(a) The need to swap programs (or parts of programs) regularly in and out of main memory.

(b) The need to allocate a small quantum of central processor time to the program currently being executed. This quantum of time is commonly called a 'time-slice'.

To appreciate the effect of these two principles and their role in time-sharing, let us consider a straightforward uniprogramming system. The principle of operation would be such that the currently active job is in memory, while other active jobs are held on backing store. When the currently active program has exhausted its quantum of time (time-slice), it is swapped out (i.e., returned to backing store) and the next job in the job queue is swapped in (loaded). Ideally, this sequence should occur with sufficient frequency so that each active job is run for a time-slice at least once during the average human reaction rate, say two seconds. In this way, each terminal user would find the system fully responsive to any demand he may make. The realization of this situation is not, if at all, readily achieved for a large number of simultaneous users.

In practice, adequate response to user demands will be dependent on such factors as the number of users on-line, the speed at which programs can be swapped, the length of the time-slice, and the processing power of the computer. In the following pages, these factors will be considered in more detail.

The foregoing method is the simplest approach to achieving time-sharing. This uniprogramming system will normally operate in the following manner. Each terminal user will, as in remote job entry, create an input file on backing store. When the terminal user gives a command to process his particular job, it will enter the active job queue. The difference when compared with remote job entry is that a program will be loaded, again usually according to a suitable scheduling algorithm, and run for a time-slice, or less than a time-slice should the program be held up for input or output. It is then swapped out and another job loaded and run. The original program, if it has not completed processing, will eventually be returned to memory and again run for a time-slice (or less). Obviously, this particular program will not be returned for processing until all the other active jobs have received their time-slice. Thus, providing the system returns the results of a job directly to the user terminal, we have achieved time-sharing. For obvious reasons, this process of continually swapping single programs and running them for short intervals of time is known as 'roll-in/roll out'. In the above, we have described a single-stream roll-in/roll-out system.

Since, in the long run, the response time for a given user is a function of the intervals between his receiving central processor time, a long time-slice causes poor overall response times. Thus, if there were ten users running with a two second time-slice, it is possible for there to be a delay of up to twenty seconds between two runs of a given job. However, the response time that a job experiences is also dependent upon the amount of terminal output generated at the last run and the length of time before the next run. For example, if thirty characters were generated to a terminal running at ten characters per second then it would take three seconds to receive the output. This output can be overlapped with other jobs running (of particular significance when considering more sophisticated methods of achieving time-sharing than single-stream roll-in/roll-out systems). The response time is from the end of this output to the beginning of the next, and is shown in Fig.3.2.

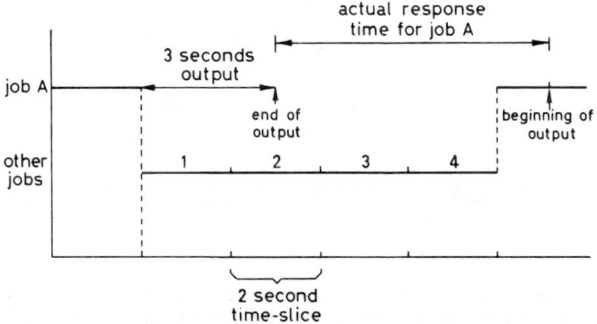

Fig. 3.2   The diagram represents 5 jobs in a system with a 2 second time-slice, indicating the actual response time for job A, allowing 3 seconds of overlapped output (no other considerations taken into account)
The above approach to achieving time-sharing has terminal activity only. It should be noted that some batch activity may be allowed. In this case, any batch jobs would be treated in exactly the same way as a terminal job. Often, any batch activity will be restricted say to sequential processing of jobs from a card reader. Obviously, any batch load placed further strain on a system that already has difficulty in achieving adequate response time.

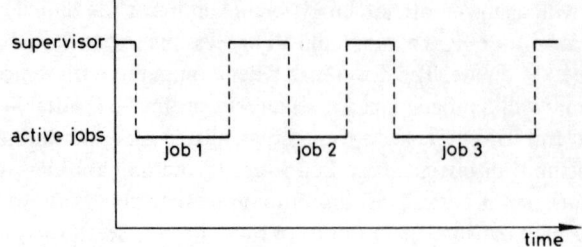

Fig. 3.3 All idle time is represented by time spent in the supervisor. Job 1 is rolled in and runs for less than a time-slice (i.e., requires input or output), Job 1 is rolled out, and Job 2 is rolled in; during this procedure the processor can perform little useful work, as indicated by the time spent in the supervisor. Job 2 is run for considerably less than a time-slice, which emphasizes the unhappy relationship which can occur between idle time and processing time. Job 3 is run for a full time-slice

Figure 3.3 illustrates how the central processor's available processing time is utilized in a single-stream roll-in/roll-out system. It can be seen quite clearly that the computer is idle for long periods of time while programs are swapped.

A method of improving the machine utilization is to introduce a distinct batch activity by partitioning the available memory into two sections, a foreground partition of a time-sliced roll-in/roll-out job stream and a background partition of batch jobs run to completion. Normally, a system of this type will operate so that the background batch partition uses only processing time while swapping is taking place in the foreground roll-in/roll-out stream. Thus, the re-

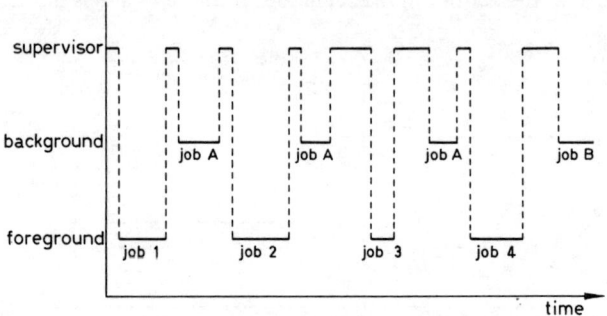

Fig. 3.4 Job 1 runs in the foreground partition for less than the time-slice. Job A is already resident and there is a short supervisor entry while Job A is initiated.
Job A runs until Job 2 is rolled in and initiated.
Job 2 runs for a full time-slice and Job A is reinitiated.
Job A runs for a short period of time and then requires input or output. Since Job 3 has not yet been fully loaded, there is much more idle time.
Job 3 is initiated and runs for considerably less than a time-slice, and, since Job A has not completed input/output, further idle time occurs.
Job A is then processed until Job 4 has been rolled in and is ready for processing.
Job 4 runs for less than a time-slice. There is again a large amount of idle time, as in the background partition Job B is being loaded in place of Job A.
Job B commences processing

sponse to terminal users is not degraded. Conversely, neither is it improved, since we have only imporved the machine utilization, not the time-sharing capability. Figure 3.4 indicates the improvement in machine utilization. In practice, as can be seen from the diagram, nothing like the total available processing time can be utilized. For example, the batch job will have to perform input and output functions which will often be initiated while swapping is taking place in the foreground partition. Figure 3.5 indicates a typical main memory layout for foreground and background operation. There are two points which should be made

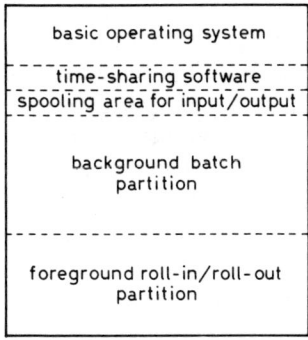

Fig. 3.5

about this type of system. Under operational conditions, one would expect that the allocation of time and priority to the background load could be controlled by the installation. This would mean that if at certain times during the day time-sharing use was low then more time, other than just foreground swapping time, could be allocated to background batch processing. This would increase batch throughput at the expense of time-sharing response. Secondly, the system should allow files created in the batch mode of operation to be accessible to the terminal users and, likewise, files created by terminal users to be available for batch use.

Without taking into account any further considerations, a distinct improvement of the system's time-sharing capability can be achieved by the use of more than one roll-in/roll-out job stream, i.e., multistream operation. Of course, both foreground/background and multistream operation employ multiprogramming techniques. However, in order to separate clearly the methods of achieving time-sharing, we prefer to keep distinct the implementation technique of dividing the available main memory into a number of fixed partitions from that of the space being allocated dynamically to a number of active programs (our definition for section 3.4). If we have a system capable of running a number (i.e., two or three) of roll-in/roll-out streams, as opposed to a single stream, then we can improve the number of simultaneous terminals supported and/or improve the response time for a given number of terminals. In either case, we shall improve the machine utilization. Let us consider the simplest case of say, two roll-in/roll-out streams plus a background partition. While swapping is taking place in one stream, processing can continue for another user in the second stream or if this stream is held up for input/output then the background batch processing can be activated. In terms of time-sharing, we must aim for a good response time to user commands in association with a method of implementation that will support as many simultaneous users as possible. On both these counts, a dual roll-in/roll-out system is more efficient than a single-stream system. For example, consider what happens to just two terminal jobs, 1 and 2. With a single stream, the operation is roll-in job 1, process (for a maximum of a time-slice), roll-out job 1, roll-in job 2, process, etc. Any output to the terminal will be handled by the time-sharing software. Now, with dual streams the operation is roll-in job 1, into the selected stream, simultaneously process job 1 while rolling-in job 2. At the end of the time-slice, process job 2 and at the same time roll-out job 1, etc. The response time to individual users is considerably improved, since the jobs are completed in a shorter time period. The improvement in machine utilization can be seen from Fig. 3.6. As with remote job entry, these approachs to time-sharing require a filing system for both terminal and batch jobs. Similarly, the establishment of active job queues and associated scheduling algorithms are fundamental to any time-sharing system.

So far, we have considered only implementation techniques; it is also important to take into account other factors.

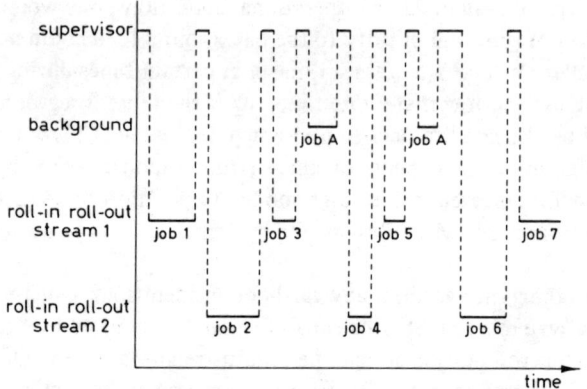

Fig. 3.6   There is a considerable reduction in idle time, since in a large number of cases there will be a job loaded and ready for processing on the termination of the previous job. The important points to note from the diagram are:

(a) Job A in the background partition is first initiated because Job 3 ran for considerably less than the time-slice (awaiting input/output) and Job 4 was not fully loaded and ready for processing

(b) There is an increase in the idle time following Jobs 4, 5, and A. As these jobs ran for a short period of time, Job 6 was not fully loaded and ready for processing

Let us first consider swapping speed. Obviously, the faster a system can swap programs in and out of main memory, thereby reducing this wasteful overhead, the more quickly individual users will be serviced and therefore the response time to users' commands and requests will be reduced.

Another factor which must be considered along with faster swapping speed is the length of the time-slice. As a result of using a faster swapping device and/or by having multistream operation, we can allow a shorter time-slice. It is important to realize the advantages of having as short a time-slice as is feasible, coincidental with maintaining sufficient processing time per job, since more jobs will be processed in a given time period. Therefore the response time a particular system can offer to a given number of users is in many ways directly proportional to the length of the time-slice. For example, let us consider again a single-stream roll-in/roll-out system. If the time-slice is, say, two seconds and there are 10 simultaneously active users, then in the worst case where all jobs run for a full time-slice, an individual user could well wait about 20 seconds before receiving a response. Now, if the time-slice were, say, 200 milliseconds, then in a similar situation the response time would be no worse than about two seconds. Therefore, although we have not taken into account all the relevant factors, we can say that those systems which implement time-sharing by swapping on the faster forms of backing store (i.e., fixed-head disc or drum), and can hence utilize a short time-slice, are in a strong position to develop a good, responsive, time-sharing system.

The response time also depends upon the amount of information that needs to be swapped. This is particularly critical for those jobs requiring compilation, since a copy of the relevant compiler must be resident in memory along with the user program. If compilation is not completed before the end of the time-slice, the current state of the user job plus the compiler must be swapped out. Likewise, a 'clean' copy of the same or a different compiler must be swapped in for the next job, should it require compilation. This situation naturally places fairly heavy demands on the swapping capability of the system. In order to alleviate this problem, those systems, in particular, which swap on the slower forms of backing store (i.e., movable head discs) use a longer time-slice and/or only time-slice the execution phase of job processing. In both cases, the aim is to increase the number of jobs which are run to completion within a single time-slice and thereby reduce the number of swaps per job. Where a system only time-slices at execution, all compilations are run to completion, which of course guarantees that there is no need to roll-out the compiler with the user job. A further improvement can be achieved, if at the end of compilation the copy of the compiler is left in a usable state for the next job, should the same compiler be required. In this case there is no need to roll-in the identical compiler with the next job. The concept of saving swapping time by ensuring that the whole compiler does not have to be returned to backing store along with the user program can be realized in a more professional manner, by ensuring that all the compilers are at any stage in a readily usable state (i.e., 're-entrant'). This means that at no time, even if compilation is unfinished during a time-slice, do we have to roll-out the compiler along with the user program, nor do we have to roll-in the same compiler if it is required for the next job. Thus, the unsatisfactory situation where the scheduling algorithm perhaps gives compilation priority and then runs compilations to completion can hopefully be avoided. It must be noted that the use of re-entrant compilers gives only limited advantages to a roll-in/roll-out system, as there is only one active program in a given stream at any one time.

Finally, the processing power of a particular computer system can have some effect on the response time and/or the number of simultaneous users a system can support. The more powerful a computer, the more processing it can carry out in a given period of time. Therefore a shorter time-slice can be utilized. If the system is using a slow-swapping device, then the advantage of more processing power is generally outweighed by the problems associated with the swapping overhead.

In summary, all the foregoing techniques will assist in improving the response time and/or the number of terminals a given system can support. Unfortunately, none can completely counteract the effect on any system that a slow-swapping device creates.

3.4 Multiprogramming and Swapping

The methods of achieving time-sharing outlined in the previous sections are in the main implemented on computer systems that were not designed with time-sharing as a major criteria. The implementation techniques suffer, particularly if no attempt has been made to utilize a very fast-swapping device, as a result of the attempts to graft time-sharing onto a basically batch-processing system. The advantage, of course, is in the relatively simple design of the software. Substantial improvements in the ability of a system to maintain a rapid response time to user commands and support more active terminals for a given response time can be achieved by developing more advanced techniques of multiprogramming than fixed-partition multistream systems.

The method of implementation when utilizing multiprogramming with swapping is to treat the available main memory of the computer system as a contiguous area in which will be held as many user jobs as there is available space. There is now no fixed partitioning or differentiation between foreground and background job processing. Figure 3.7 illustrates a typical main memory layout. In this case, there are five jobs indicated, although this could be any number, depending on the individual job sizes and the size of the available main memory.

With multiprogramming with swapping each job is given a time-slice and will be run for this time-slice or until it requires input or output, whichever is sooner. At this point, another resident job can be activated. The more jobs there are in memory at any one time the better the chance that the operating system will be able to find an executable job (i.e., one not awaiting input or output). Any

```
┌─────────────────────┐
│   complete          │
│ operating system    │
├─────────────────────┤
│      job 1          │
├─────────────────────┤
│      job 2          │
├─────────────────────┤
│      job 3          │
├─────────────────────┤
│      job 4          │
├─────────────────────┤
│      job 5          │
├─────────────────────┤
│/////////////////////│
└─────────────────────┘
```

Fig. 3.7 The shaded area represents unused main memory locations insufficient to load any jobs currently in the job queue

swapping required to bring into memory jobs awaiting processing can be initiated by the operating system and continue in parallel with processing the current job. If there is insufficient space available for the incoming job, it is a function of the operating system to swap out a resident job to make room. In many ways, the basic process of multiprogramming and swapping can be viewed as an extension of the principles of multistream operations outlined earlier; the fundamental difference is that main memory space can be allocated dynamically to jobs.

Let us now consider the situation regarding the processing of batch jobs. We now no longer have a distinct background batch-processing stream and thus, in general, batch jobs will be treated in exactly the same way as the interactive terminal jobs (i.e., they will be run for a time-slice and swapped in and out as necessary in exactly the same manner as interactive tasks). This situation can cause two problems. Firstly, the throughput of batch jobs will not be as good as with a partitioned system, since batch jobs are competing on a par with all other jobs. Therefore, the more interactive jobs a system is supporting at any time, the less frequently batch jobs will be run. Secondly, large batch jobs (in terms of main memory size) will noticeably increase the response time to terminal users while the job is resident. The available space is greatly reduced and fewer terminal jobs can be held in main memory. (Note that the same effect will result of course if a large terminal job is introduced into the system.) Also, in order to make room for a large job, the operating system may well have to swap out a number of smaller terminal jobs, again effecting the response time that a system can maintain. To improve the situation, many systems utilize more sophisticated job-scheduling algorithms. For example, a typical solution is to increase the time-slice for large and/or long jobs and at the same time reduce the priority in the job queue so that these jobs are run less frequently. Thus, these jobs run for longer when in memory but are not swapped in and out as frequently as the smaller jobs. Typically, the large, long-running jobs are of a batch-processing nature; by introducing this type of scheduling algorithm their effect is isolated rather than continually degrading the response time of a system.

The conclusions we can draw so far are as follows:

(a) An increase in the number of large jobs will increase the terminal response time, whereas a loading of small jobs will show a significant decrease in response time.

(b) Any increase in available main memory immediately improves the performance of a multiprogramming system, since more jobs can be held in memory at any one time. This is a particularly important consideration when evaluating the expansion capabilities of time-sharing systems. For example, many fixed-partition systems (as discussed earlier) are limited to two or three partitions. Thus, enhancement of the system in terms of main memory gives no added benefit other than the ability to run larger jobs.

As mentioned earlier, a multiprogramming environment requires fairly sophisticated control software within the operating system, generally in association with special hardware. One reason is that, since the available main memory is allocated dynamically when a job is swapped out and then subsequently swapped in again for further processing, it is extremely unlikely that it will be loaded into the same location in main memory, since in this dynamic environment demand on the space is changing as the jobs change. Thus, the system must be capable of allocating jobs and running them from any position in main memory. In order to achieve this, the system must make use of special relocation registers. Similarly, since there can be a large number of jobs randomly distributed in memory at any one time, it is absolutely vital that the system maintains an effective memory protection system. This is to ensure that an active job in no way interferes with an area of main memory currently occupied by another user job, thereby perhaps corrupting program or data areas of this particular job. (The details of relocation and memory protection are more appropriately discussed in chapter 4.) It should be obvious that the fixed-partition approach alleviates the problems main memory management, since all jobs are run from the same fixed area of main memory. In order to protect the operating system, it is necessary to use relocation and protection registers as with a multiprogramming system.

Another problem created by the concept of multiprogramming is that of main memory fragmentation. Since jobs are of varying sizes, and as a large number of jobs are swapped in and out, unusable gaps appear in main memory between jobs. Figure 3.8 indicates this situation, and in general, a process of 'cleaning up' the main memory will be necessary. The current jobs in main memory are moved up and grouped together so that a contiguous area is left vacant, as shown in Fig. 3.9. An alternative approach is to ignore the problem altogether, on the assumption that as job processing continues the variability of job sizes will ensure the level of main memory wastage is kept within reasonable limits. This argument is certainly valid where there are a large number of interactive users, and in particular if there are plenty of small jobs to be processed (which is of course often the case in time-sharing).

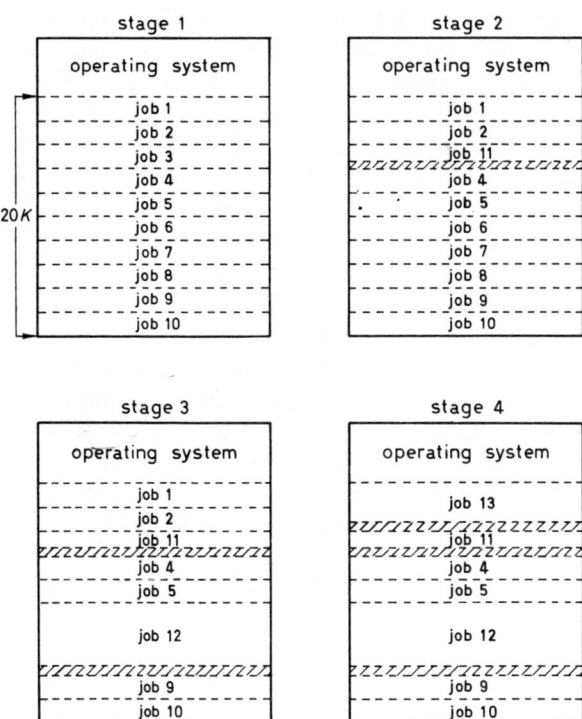

Fig. 3.8 Assume 20K words of available main memory. Shading represents unusable areas of 1K, assuming that there are no jobs of 1K or less in the current job queues

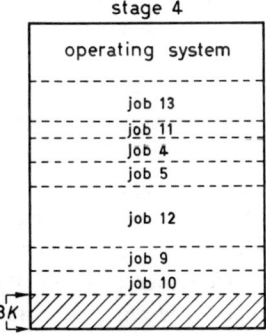

Fig. 3.9 Stage 4 from Fig. 3.8, after reorganization. If there is a job of 3K or less in the current job queue, it can immediately be swapped in without swapping out any other jobs to make room

55

As we have seen in earlier sections, the amount of data that has to be swapped between main memory and backing store (even when a fast-swapping device is used) plays an important part in the ability of a system to maintain good response times. In a multiprogramming environment, we are in an ideal position to reduce the amount of data that needs to be swapped, if the system allows users to share standard software modules such as compilers (i.e., using re-entrant coding). For example, during an interactive session, a large number of user jobs will require compilation and of these many will wish to utilize the same compiler. If a given compiler is re-entrant then when a job which is using the compiler reaches, say, the end of its time-slice and is a candidate for swapping, only the user program need be swapped out and not the compiler as well. This, then, significantly reduces the amount of data that needs to be swapped. Also, another user job can immediately make use of the same compiler, since the principle of re-entrant coding is that it is always in a 'clean' state ready to be used at any stage. The use of re-entrant coding requires a fairly sophisticated memory protection system which will distinguish between reading and writing in various parts of the memory. It is necessary to isolate those parts of the main memory where a re-entrant compiler may be resident and ensure that reading is the only mode of access permitted to prevent a user job from corrupting the compiler. Another benefit gained by using re-entrant software is that is increases the amount of available main memory to user jobs. Each individual job requiring compilation does not have to have its own copy of a compiler. Therefore, more jobs can be held in memory at one time, and thus response times can be reduced. (Re-entrant coding is discussed further in chapter 4.) If the number of re-entrant compilers available at certain times is restricted, the overall performance of the system can be greatly enhanced.

It is important to realize that systems which utilize re-entrant compilers are in an excellent position to have a short time-slice, since the swapping overhead is reduced. Therefore jobs are run more frequently and thus response times should be reduced and/or the number of simultaneous users a given system can support increased.

So far throughout this chapter, we have emphasized the importance of having a fast swapping device in order to implement time-sharing effectively. However, no matter what method is used to achieve time-sharing, the number and capacity of the input/output channels between backing store and the processor also play an important role in relation to the time-sharing performance of a given system. For example, if we have a system which has a fast swapping device and subsidiary file store (say two or three replaceable discs) sharing one input/output channel, then at one time data can only be transferred to or from one of the backing store devices. We would thus not be in a position to take advantage of, say, a typical situation where one job is being transferred to or from the swapping device while at the same time another job is simultaneously moving results to an output file, since one or other of the data transfers would have to wait until the first transfer was complete.

No matter how sophisticated the system software, time-sharing capability will be restricted by the fact that there is only one route available for the transfer of data. Now, if the swapping device were on a separate channel to the file storage devices then the above clash of data transfers would be avoided. In general, when one is evaluating a particular time-sharing system proposal, it is vital to ensure that there are adequate channels specified in order to maximize the amount of data transfer overlap that can be achieved, coincidental with the method by which time-sharing is implemented. For example, if we are considering a straightforward uniprogramming system than an increase in the number of available channels will have little affect on system performance.

Finally, remember that the more sophisticated the method of time-sharing implementation, the more sophisticated the operating system has to be in order to exercise the necessary control. More time has to be spent in the operating system and therefore software overheads are greater than with a simple approach to time-sharing implementation. Also, the more sophisticated the requirements of the operating system the larger it becomes, thereby reducing the amount of main memory available to users.

3.5 Paging

As we have seen in the previous section, the use of multiprogramming and swapping brings many advantages in terms of improved performance, but it also brings other problems which must be overcome if the system is to be as efficient as possible, in particular the problems of relocation of programs, main memory fragmentation, and the need to establish contiguous location in order to process a program. To overcome these problems of main memory management, we may introduce the concept of *paging*.

Let us first consider memory mapping. With this approach the available main memory is subdivided into a convenient number of page frames, generally of a fixed size (currently of the order of 500 or 1000 words). When a program is loaded, it does not now have to go into a contiguous area of memory, but is

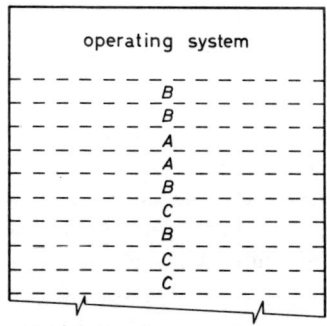

Fig. 3.10 Only part of the main memory is shown for simplicity. Each space between the dotted lines represents a page

instead allocated to available page frames (sufficient to hold the program), which may be scattered anywhere in memory. Figure 3.10 indicates how the main memory may be arranged at some point in time to hold the three programs *A*, *B*, and *C*.

This approach to memory allocation is more complex than the traditional form of multiprogramming as outlined earlier, and hence requires both software and hardware enhancements. It is necessary to subdivide the normal address field of a program instruction into two parts, the first part of which determines the page number and the second the line within a page. Thus we have divided the program and its data blocks into pages. Consecutive pages of a program will not necessarily go into consecutive page frames in main memory. Thus there must be a mechanism to relate the program pages to the page frames, and this can be achieved by maintaining permanently in main memory a *page table*, which is utilized by the program currently being processed. This gives the page frames into which the program pages have been loaded. The user of the system is totally unaware of these processes, and that the whole operation is entirely automatic.

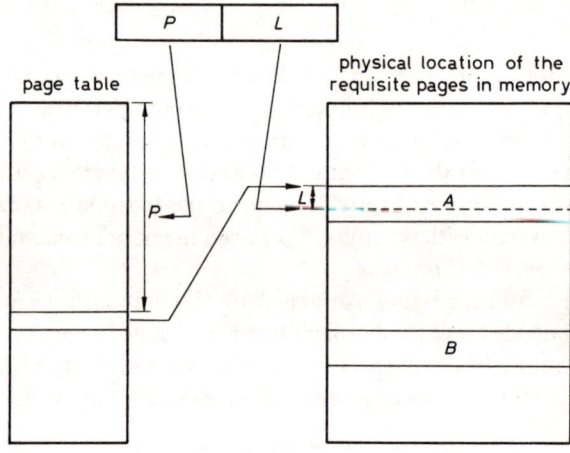

Fig. 3.11

Figure 3.11 indicates how this process operates. Suppose a program occupies two non-contiguous page frames, *A* and *B*. When an address is decoded, the page number '*P*' is used to reference the page table and hence extract the address of the page frame containing the required page (in this case *A*). The line number '*L*' is then used to locate the absolute address required.

From the foregoing, the reader should be aware that if the page table is referenced from main memory, two cycles would be required to address any requisite word, one cycle to access the page table and one to retrieve the required word. Since the page table is not large, we should expect to find that fast hardware registers of their equivalent were provided for the table. If this is done, there should be little noticeable degradation in the performance of a given system.

As we have already indicated, the advantage of the approach outlined above is that a program is conveniently subdivided and can be placed in any available page frame. However, it is sometimes claimed that a further advantage of such a system is that it entirely eliminates the problem of main memory wastage—this it certainly does not. It may well assist in slightly reducing the wastage, but what is perhaps more true is that it obscures the problem, since wastage will occur within page frames. It will be very rare that the main memory requirements of a program will correspond exactly to an integral number of pages, and thus many page frames will be only partly used.

As has been pointed out in earlier sections, one of the problems which can cause difficulty in achieving maximum performance from a time-sharing system is the amount of data flow between main memory and backing storage. An extension to the concept of memory mapping, known as *paging*, can make a significant contribution in easing this problem.

With paging, instead of the whole user program being mapped into main memory, only a few of the currently active program pages are in memory at one time. When an attempt is made to access a word in a non-resident page, the call is trapped and the supervisor entered; the supervisor then proceeds to load the requisite page and update the page table. This approach therefore offers to a time-sharing system two distinct advantages. Since a page of a program need not be loaded until it is actually needed, the data flow between backing store and main memory should be reduced. Also, as the system is only holding in the available main memory parts of active programs, this will mean that in many cases more user programs (i.e., that part of the user program which is currently being processed) can be held in memory at one time. If paging is effective in this way, the time-sharing performance of a given system will be considerably enhanced.

However, the concept of paging does bring with it specific problems such as determining an effective algorithm for page replacement and maintaining an appropriate page-fetching mechanism. These problems are discussed in the next chapter.

Memory mapping using fast hardware registers offers certain distinct advantages in a swapping system. It helps solve the problem of relocation of programs and avoids having to establish contiguous areas of main memory in order to do this. Theoretically, the case for paging is even stronger, in that it should reduce the data traffic between main memory and backing store and at the same time noticeably increase the number of users that can be held in the available main memory. However, the system management involved in manipulating the pages will cause a high overhead. Further experience is necessary before we can say that the penalty of increased system overhead justifies sophisticated paging techniques within the environment of time-sharing. It is interesting to note that the more successful commercial time-sharing systems have not at this time used paging but have relied upon a fast swapping device. Lastly, it may well be that as the price of main memory falls other completely new techniques will evolve which do not rely on space-saving devices such as paging.

3.6 Communications

So far in this chapter, we have been concerned with the various methods by which time-sharing can be achieved, without considering how each user terminal may be connected to the system. It is vital that an efficient means of connecting a large number of terminals to a system is utilized. The device which performs this function is commonly known as a multiplexer, used either alone or in conjunction with a separate communications processor, as we shall see later.

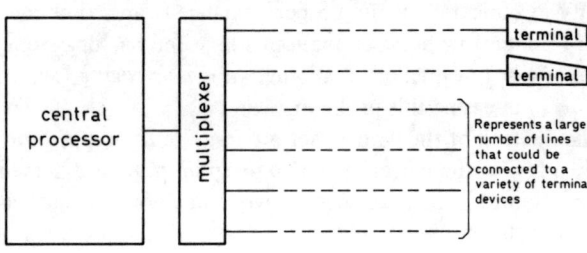

Fig. 3.12

Figure 3.12 indicates the conventional arrangement of terminals, multiplexer, and main processor. It is important to note that the terminals are connected to the multiplexer over their individual lines and that the multiplexer is connected to the main processor by a *single* input/output channel.

The multiplexer functions basically as a switch that scans all the terminal interfaces sequentially. When a character is detected, the multiplexer passes this to the main processor along with the associated line number for identification. When the character transfer is complete, the next line in sequence is tested to see if it is active and whether there is a character to be transferred, and so on. Similarly, on output a character is transferred from the main processor to the multiplexer, which selects the correct terminal by again utilizing the line number associated with the outgoing character. Also, into the multiplexer it is necessary to build interface logic for each line over and above the relatively simple scanning mechanism. Along with each line, for example, it will be necessary to have a character buffer plus specific line-sampling logic. These components will be duplicated for every line. For a limited number of lines, the cost of duplication is negligible when compared with the processor interface costs. As we shall see later, this is not necessarily the best solution when the number of lines increases.

Obviously, there must be a restriction on the number of lines a multiplexer can support, as it must be capable of servicing all the available terminals simultaneously, during one scan cycle, without losing any characters. In order to appreciate a multiplexer's capacity, let us consider briefly the timing of a scanning sequence. Typically, it might take four microseconds to step onto the next line and another four microseconds to test that line (i.e., eight microseconds per scanning step). It might take 70 microseconds to perform the character transfer. With a multiplexer having a maximum capacity of 63 lines (which is fairly common), the reader will find, if he or she cares to do the arithmetic, that this typical multiplexer can safely operate at 200 characters per second per line when all 63 lines are simultaneously active. Obviously, higher speeds of data transfer are possible if fewer lines are active simultaneously.

It is perhaps as well at this point to define the difference between asynchronous and synchoronous transmission. With asynchronous transmission, characters are transmitted at random intervals. It is therefore necessary for the receiving device to synchronize onto each character as it arrives. Each character transmitted is made up of a serial bit stream consisting of a start bit, data bits, and a stop bit. The start bit is used to indicate the arrival of a character and to initiate bit sampling using some suitable clock mechanism. The stop bit indicates the end of a character. Asynchronous transmission is ideally suited to electromechanical devices such as teletypes and is therefore a particularly common mode of transmission in time-sharing. With synchronous transmission, the transmitting and receiving media are driven by the same or equivalent timing devices. Thus an entire block data can by synchronized rather than individual characters. This facility, along with the use of synchronous data sets (modems), has made this method of transmission particularly suitable for the higher speeds of data transfer over voice grade lines and above. The buffered terminals such as card readers, line printers, and visual display units, are typically suited to this mode of transmission.

With asynchronous transmission it will be necessary to incorporate a clock mechanism within the multiplexer, for either each line or a group of lines operating at the same speed, in order to correctly sample each data bit as it arrives at an individual interface. This is not a requirement of synchronous transmission since there is no need for bit synchronization, as the data set will supply all the necessary timing.

The approach to multiplexing a number of user terminals outlined above has two disadvantages in that the communications software must be held and operated upon in the main processor. If the lack of power in the processor is a contributing factor in maintaining adequate response times, removing communication handling from the main processor should improve response times. Removing the communications software will also make available more space for a multiprogramming mix. For example, the main processor will have to monitor the communication lines, collect characters into complete messages (e.g., a line of a program) and perform any initial editing necessary prior, say, to adding the message to the filing system. These activities represent software overheads which could detract from the time-sharing performance of a given system. The solution in such cases is to remove as much as possible of the communication software from the main processor.

Figure 3.13 illustrates the current trend in communications handling. A second small computer is introduced between the main computer and the multiplexer. This intermediary computer now acts as a communications processor.

Let us now consider the advantages to be gained by utilizing a communications processor.

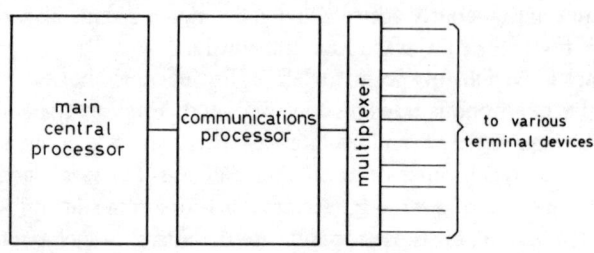

Fig. 3.13

Possibly the major advantage is that, by having a small computer as the basic communications handler, a large part of the associated software can be brought into this 'front-end' processor, thereby removing a substantial part of the communications software overhead from the main computer. Also, since we now have a programmable communications handler we have the opportunity of using it as a straightforward character buffering system (i.e., in the same way as if it were a conventional multiplexer) or as a message-buffering system. In the latter case, characters are assembled into complete messages and can be edited prior to onward transmission to the main computer. This means that, firstly, these functions are carried out independently of the main system, and that, secondly, the main processor is only interrupted when a message is complete instead of at the receipt of each character. Obviously, this approach considerably reduces the communication software overhead placed on the main system. The message-buffering approach is of particular significance if a given system is effectively to handle synchronous transmission to and from the faster remote devices.

As can be seen from Fig. 3.13, in front of the communications processor we still require a multiplexer to perform at least the basic function of scanning the terminal interfaces. But we no longer require the duplicated interface logic and character buffers of a conventional hardware multiplexer, since the communications processor can undertake these functions. In some systems, for asynchronous transmission, the multiplexer will still be required to perform bit synchronization via a clock mechanism. As indicated earlier, this requires, at best, a different clock for each different line speed, where the system is supporting a variety of terminal devices operating at different transmission rates.

An alternative approach is to use the communications processor to establish and maintain line synchronization. This technique does require a communications-orientated processor with an instruction speed capable of handling many lines. An advantage is that the multiplexer functions as little more than a line scanner, and therefore the cost of adding lines to the system is very low. Also, since line synchronization is now handled by the communications processor and is under program control, it is possible to accept various transmission rates. This ability can play an important part in ensuring maximum utilization of available lines, since it is not now necessary to assign specific lines to set transmission rates in order to be correctly sampled by the clock mechanism related to the particular line.

This point is perhaps best illustrated by an example. Suppose a time-sharing bureau wishes to service three different terminal devices operating at, say, 110, 150, and 200 baud (bits per second) and the total number of lines available is to be 60. If line synchronization is not under program control then it is necessary to assign three separate hunting groups (a consecutive series of telephone numbers which can be reached by dialling the first; the telephone equipment selects the first available line), each serving a specific line speed. The customer then must dial one of three numbers, depending on the terminal he is using. The logical choice in this case would be to have a twenty-line hunting group for each of the possible line speeds (110, 150, and 200 baud). If, at a given period in time, the system were serving 20 users operating at 110 baud, 10 at 150 baud, and 5 at 200 baud, then, if another customer wishes to dial in using a 110 baud terminal, the system cannot service him even though over 40% of the lines are free. If the line speed is under program control, then only one hunting group is necessary. When a customer dials in, the system can determine the baud rate and proceed to service the terminal by selecting the appropriate clock (timer) and utilize this in conjunction with line sampling under program control. Hence all 60 lines are available to any user regardless of transmission rate, obviously within the bounds of line capacity and available clock mechanisms.

With the approach to using a communications processor as outlined above, one is taking a far greater percentage of processor time in order to service a line, and therefore this does place a further restriction on the maximum speed of lines it can service.

In some systems, a further advantage can be gained in the use of a communications processor by allowing it to have access to part of the main filing system. In this case, for example, source files could be edited and stored in the filing system without reference to the main computer. The main computer would be interrupted only when a file was complete and ready for processing, thus reducing even further the software overheads placed on the main computer. This approach, of course, does require fairly sophisticated communications software in the 'front-end' processor. It is perhaps worth pointing out that in some cases this approach is used to improve even further the time-sharing capability of an already powerful system. Alternatively, it is a technique used to enhance the performance of a simple time-sharing system.

An example of utilizing a communications processor in the way that has been outlined above is in the G.E. time-sharing systems which employ a Datanet 30 as the communications processor. Another example is the Honeywell 1648 system, which uses three processors, a DDP 416 to perform the basic multiplexing operation, one DDP 516 which acts as the control computer performing the editing and building of source files, and a second DDP 516 which acts as the job processor. Both the 516s have access to the filing system.

Before completing this section, it is perhaps worth defining the types of communication lines available. They can be classified into three types: simplex, half-duplex, and duplex.

(a) A simplex line is one in which data can be transmitted in one direction and one direction only, obviously unusable in terms of time-sharing.

(b) A half-duplex line is one in which data can be transmitted in either direction, but only in one direction at a time.

(c) A duplex line is one in which data can be transmitted in either direction simultaneously.

In duplex operation, as each character is composed at the terminal keyboard it is transmitted down the line to the systen and it is echoed back to the terminal and printed. This offers certain advantages in the time-sharing environment. Firstly, it is possible to arrange for the system to prevent passwords printing at the terminal during the logging-in procedure. In this case, the system does not echo back password characters, but instead stores and checks the password without printing it at the terminal. Obviously, 'non-printing' passwords are an important security procedure which can greatly assist in ensuring that each user's password to the system is not easily obtained by others. Secondly, the terminal operator is not dependent on the speed of the system and can in fact be typing ahead of the actual printing. In the case of a good operator, this can prevent frustration occurring due to a foreknowledge of a tedious or lengthy interaction such as occurs at login time. Typing ahead can also have the disadvantage in some cases of causing disorientation, since what is being typed is not being directly printed.

In half-duplex operation, printing must be directly related to typing, since it is impossible to echo back characters. Thus, a user's password is printed and available for all to see. However, most systems will attempt to overcome this problem by causing the system to overscore or mask the password area. This is achieved by printing a string of obliterating characters, over which the password is subsequently typed. A further problem associated with half-duplex operation is that while the system is outputting to the terminal the user is unable to interrupt, since there is only a single line. A solution is to provide a regular pause during output (say at the end of the line) to enable the user to send 'break' character which causes the program to stop and hence prevent further output.

Finally, if one is evaluating the communications capabilities of a given time-sharing system there are two further points which should be considered. The first is the necessity of having automatic telephone answering if the system is to support more than a very limited number of simultaneous remote users. This can be achieved fairly easily by hardware, and does alleviate the problems of a large manual switchboard. It is also important to have an automatic disconnect facility such that if a user replaces the telephone without going through the standard logging-off procedure the system will tidy-up behind him and real-locate the communication channel.

A line failure should be treated in the same way. Automatic disconnect is a software problem because it is necessary to:

(a) recognize the disappearance of the carrier (a hardware function), and

(b) undertake software recovery to cause automatic log-off of that user within a standard procedure.

Normally, since the system cannot distinguish between failure to log-off and line failure, a common approach is for the system to wait a predetermined period of time (say three minutes). Thus, if the same user comes back on again, the system can continue processing once identification has been established, otherwise the user is automatically logged-off the system.

4 Design Features

> He couldn't design a cathedral without making it look like the First Supernatural Bank.
>
> Eugene O'Neill

4.1 Interrupts and Multiprogramming

One of the characteristics of modern machines is that the peripheral units operate independently of, and concurrently with, the central processor (CPU), once the instructions to initiate the input/output operation have been issued by the processor. Since input/output operations are common to all user jobs, and since the programming required to handle peripherals is not something users wish to be concerned with, it is usual for there to be a set of routines, which we shall collectively call the supervisor, to handle input and output. In the simplest case, the user program would request an input or output operation (throughout this section input and output are treated as being logically the same) and the supervisor would perform the operation on the user's behalf before returning control to the user. This situation is shown in Fig.4.1. All that is required in this instance is a convention for passing parameters and a standard entry point to the supervisor. In this case, the supervisor differs from other subroutines called by the users only in that it is resident in a fixed area of main memory. Since the supervisor waits for the peripheral to complete its transfer, it is obvious that time

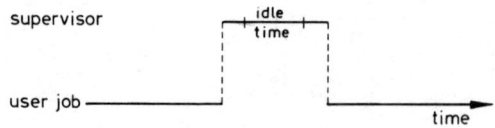

Fig. 4.1

is wasted during this period, as the processor is doing nothing useful once it has set the peripheral in action. On completion of the transfer, the supervisor checks to see that the operation was successful and, if so, transfers control back to the user program.

An improvement on this situation is for the supervisor to provide two separate routines, one to initiate the input/output transfers, and another to tidy up on completion of the transfers. In this case, it is necessary for the peripheral to be able to signal that the transfer has completed so that the termination routine can be entered. This signal is called an 'interrupt'. The situation is shown in Fig. 4.2. Since a request for input/output and an interrupt from a peripheral

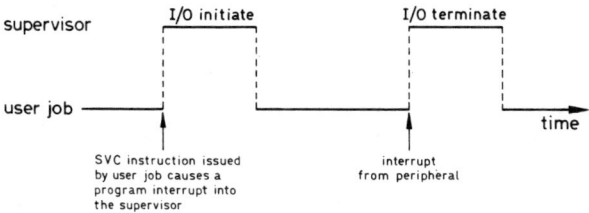

Fig. 4.2

both cause an entry into the supervisor, the supervisor deals with both types of entry in the same way. Thus, an input/output request is an interrupt generated by program. To distinguish the two kinds of interrupts, we shall call an input/output request a supervisor call (SVC). Although Fig. 4.2 shows that the CPU is now fully occupied, it is not the true picture. We have shown the supervisor returning control to the user program following initiation, and the user job continuing to run until the (peripheral) interrupt occurs. However, in many cases, and particularly when inputting, the user program may have nothing to do until the data is received. Thus, although it is now *possible* to transfer control back to the user program immediately following the initiation of the transfer, and thus give the CPU some useful work, it is unlikely that the user job has sufficient work (if any at all) to keep the processor occupied for the duration of the transfer. In order to improve CPU utilization, and also to increase the likelihood of other peripherals being brought into action, the concept of multiprogramming is introduced. In the simplest case, this consists of two programs being in main memory at the same time. Whenever one program is unable to run, owing to delay caused by an input/output operation, control is transferred to the second. This is shown in Fig. 4.3. At time t_1 user job A issues an SVC for an input/output operation and the supervisor, after analysing the cause of the interrupt, checking the parameters, and checking that the peripheral unit is available, sets the transfer in motion. At time t_2, the supervisor transfers control to user job B. User job B runs until the input/output operation terminates, and generates an interrupt. The supervisor analyses the interrupt to determine the cause and then,

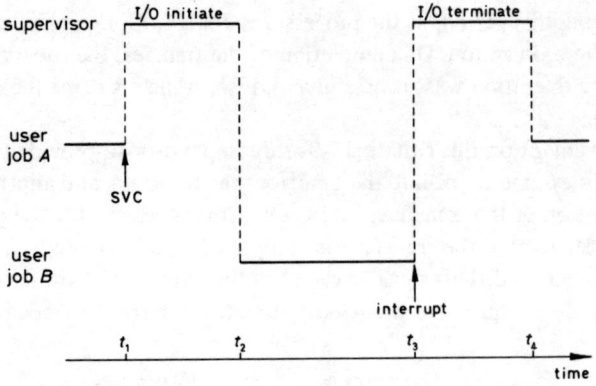

Fig. 4.3

having identified it, checks that the operation was successful by testing the status information returned by the peripheral control unit, and then returns control to user job A (as shown) or user job B, both of which are in a position to run. (Scheduling is discussed in the next section.)

Let us now extend our example a little to the situation where user job B issues an SVC after time t_2 but before time t_3. In this case, both user jobs will be held up waiting for an input/output operation to terminate and we are back to the situation where the CPU becomes idle. The situation is shown in Fig. 4.4.

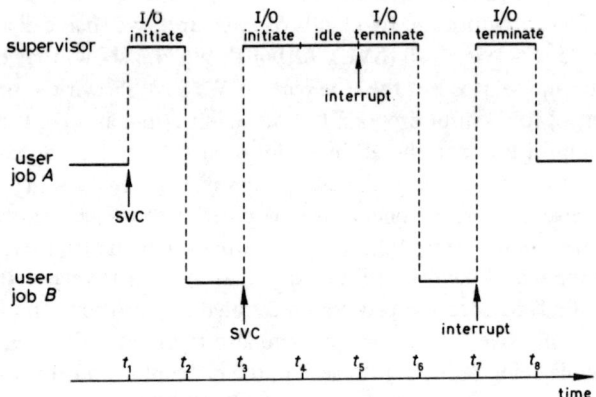

Fig. 4.4

At time t_1, user job A issues an SVC and the supervisor initiates the transfer and runs user job B from time t_2. At time t_3, user job B issues an SVC (for a different peripheral, we shall assume, to that in use by job A) and the supervisor initiates this transfer. At time t_4, there is nothing to do since both jobs A and B are awaiting for a peripheral to terminate before proceeding. At time t_5, an interrupt is received from a peripheral. The supervisor has the task of identifying the peripheral that caused the interrupt, checking that the operation was successful, and associating with this peripheral the job which is awaiting this completion—Fig. 4.4 assumes that the peripheral was that associated with user job B. Although the transfer for job B was initiated after that for job A, if the peripheral associated with job B is the faster of the two, it is possible for it to finish earlier. At time t_6, user job B is restarted and interrupted at time t_7. The supervisor identifies this as belonging to job A and restarts job A (it could equally well continue to run job B—we shall discuss the problem of scheduling jobs in a multiprogramming environment in the next section).

We see that even with two jobs it is possible for the CPU to be idle. To attempt to overcome this, we can introduce more jobs under the control of the supervisor on the assumption that the more jobs there are the more likelihood there is that the supervisor can find a job not held up for input/output. The price of introducing more jobs in this way (always assuming that there is sufficient main memory to do so) is that the supervisor has more work to do in administering the extra jobs, with the result that some of the time spent by the CPU is on administrative tasks and is in some senses non-productive in that it is not obeying user programs. However, the gain should handsomely exceed the loss.

We have shown in Figs. 4.3 and 4.4 that at time t_2 the supervisor transfers control to user job B, having previously been running user job A. Since in general there will be a single set of hardware registers, such as accumulators, index registers, and the program counter available to a user job, it is obvious that the supervisor must protect each user job's copy of these registers. The usual action is to copy the contents of all sharable registers into standard locations within the user job's area whenever a job is interrupted, either by the job issuing an SVC or by a peripheral interrupt.

One of the problems the supervisor must overcome is in dealing with the occurrence of two (or more) simultaneous interrupts, or what amounts to the same thing, the occurrence of an interrupt while a prior interrupt is being analysed. The usual technique is to give the supervisor the ability to inhibit interrupts for short periods. While interrupts are inhibited, any subsequent peripheral interrupts will be remembered, so when the supervisor turns off the inhibit mechanism, an interrupt will immediately be recognized. It is clear that the supervisor has privileges not available to user programs; in particular, the supervisor is able to inhibit interrupts. If the inhibiting of interrupts is accomplished by obeying a machine instruction, it would obviously be possible for a user to generate the appropriate instruction code and attempt to obey it. The hardware must in some way detect that it is obeying a user program rather than the supervisor. This is accomplished by having two states in which the machine operates—user mode and supervisor mode. In user mode, attempting to execute a privileged instruction causes a change of state and is a program-generated interrupt. The supervisor will, on recognizing the cause of the interrupt, deal with it by generating an error message and removing the job from the job mix.

Thus, there are two types of program-generated interrupts—an SVC, which is a request for supervisor to do something on behalf of the user, and an illegal action by the program, which the supervisor must deal with in order to ensure that it remains in control of the machine. Both of these program-generated interrupts cause a transfer of control to a fixed location within the supervisor. In general, all interrupts are handled in this way. The supervisor then analyses the cause of the interrupt. On some machines, all interrupts are trapped to the same location. On others, the type of interrupt determines the location in supervisor to which control is transferred. In the latter case, the hardware has carried out the first stage of the interrupt analysis.

The class of illegal actions extends beyond obeying (or attempting to obey) privileged instructions, and includes obeying instruction codes not within the defined set, attempting to address main memory outside the area allocated to the job (another of supervisor's tasks is to protect each user job from the others and we shall discuss this later), and program errors such as floating point overflow (i.e., generating a number too big to be represented in the standard form).

A change of state from user mode to supervisor mode may thus occur as a result of a peripheral interrupt, an SVC, or an illegal program action. A change from supervisor mode to user mode is accomplished only by issuing the appropriate privileged instruction in supervisor mode. We have said earlier that there is usually a single set of registers shared by all users of the machine, and this often includes the supervisor. An improvement in performance is achieved by giving each state its own set of registers, so that register dumping and restoring can be kept to a minimum. With a machine with two sets of registers, *(a)* registers would not be dumped at each entry to the supervisor, and *(b)* the user registers are only changed when control is transferred to a new user job. A further refinement is to recognise that the supervisor has two distinct functions: *(a)* the analysis of interrupts and the selection of the routines to deal with the interrupt, and *(b)* the execution of the routines selected. If a machine is designed with three states rather than two—let us call them states $S1$, $S2$, and $S3$—such that interrupts cause an entry into the $S3$ state, supervisor routines run in the $S2$ state, and user programs run in the $S1$ state, a further improvement in efficiency can be achieved. In state $S3$, the machine will run with interrupts inhibited and will have maximum privileges. In state $S2$, certain privileged operations such as the ability to mask interrupts, read, and write to the entire main memory, will be allowed. in state $S1$, the user will have no privileges. Each state will have its own set of registers, and register dumping will be kept to a minimum. Not all states will have, or need, the same number of registers, in general, the $S3$ state will require the least number of registers and the $S1$ state the most. Neither supervisor state will require floating point registers, for example.

The supervisor must be able to handle multiple requests for input/output on the same device. This is particularly true in the case of drum and disc. The solution is for the input/output initiate routine to place the request on a queue for the peripheral and then to see if the peripheral is busy or not. If it is busy, the supervisor exits to the next task. If it is not busy, then the initiate routine takes the request at the head of the queue (which will be the one just placed there if the queue was previously empty) and initiates the appropriate transfer. Figure 4.5 shows the action of a supervisor in this area in more detail. Let us assume

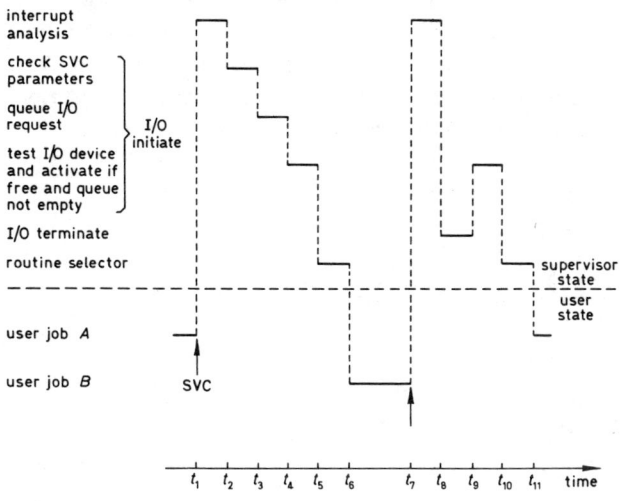

Fig. 4.5

that only the one peripheral is active. At time t_1, user job A issues an SVC for input/output. The interrupt is analysed and recognized as an SVC, and at time t_2 the routine to check that the appropriate parameters have been supplied is entered. At t_3, the input/output request is put on the queue for the relevant peripheral. The queue prior to this may have been empty or not and the peripheral at that time may be in use or not. At time t_4, a routine is entered to test the availability of the peripheral and the state of the queue. Since in this case we have just entered something in the queue, it depends only on the availability of the peripheral. If the peripheral is free, the routine sets it going. If it is busy, the routine exits. Later in time, an interrupt will be received to indicate that the peripheral has completed the current operation and the routine to activate the device will be entered again. At time t_5, the selector is entered to decide which job to run next. At time t_6, user job B is entered and in this simple example runs until an interrupt is received at time t_7. The interrupt is analysed and recognized as a peripheral terminate, and at t_8 the appropriate terminate routine in entered. At t_9, the routine to activate the device is entered again. This ensures that if there are entries in the queue for the peripheral that has just terminated they will be serviced. Following this, the selector is entered and user job A is entered at t_{11}.

In Fig. 4.2, we saw the supervisor returning control to the user program immediately following an SVC from that program. This is the alternative approach to immediate suspension of a user program following an SVC. If control is returned to the user program issuing the SVC, it is necessary to give the user program the facility to indicate that it cannot proceed until the input/output operation has completed. Only on receiving this information will the supervisor suspend the job and transfer control to another. This situation is shown in Fig. 4.6. It is the same as Fig. 4.5 up to time t_6, at which point user job A is rerun until t_7, when job A issues an SVC, indicating that the job should be suspended until the input/output operation requested at time t_1 has completed. At time t_{11}, job B is set running until the peripheral interrupt is received at time t_{12}, from which point the procedure is again the same as in Fig. 4.5 from t_7.

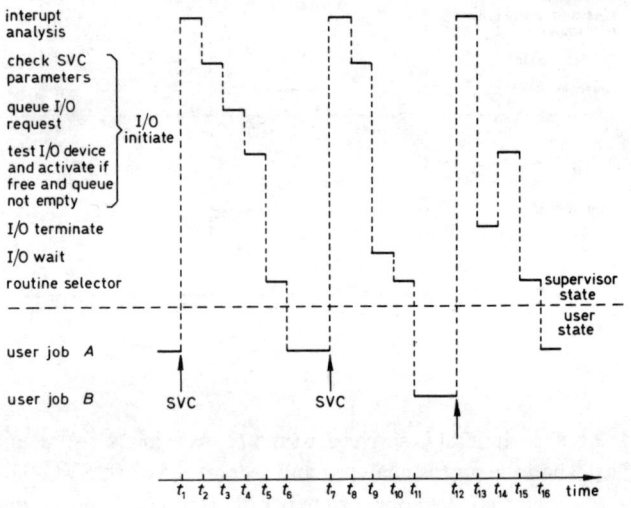

Fig. 4.6

The supervisor, in summary, is a collection of routines for organizing multiprogramming and dealing with all input and output operations. The supervisor will be permanently resident in main memory. The interrupt analysis part of the supervisor is a combination of hardware and software. In principle, a great deal of the work of the supervisor could be done by hardware, but if too much is handled by hardware flexibility is lost, and adding new peripherals, particularly non-standard peripherals, can become a major task involving the addition of new hardware for a new version of the supervisor.

Relocation and protection. So far, we have said nothing about the problem of protection in a multiprogramming environment. With a number of programs in main memory, it is essential that one program does not interfere with another and, in particular, that no program violates the supervisor. The most common way of providing such security is to make use of a pair of hardware registers called *base and limit registers* (also known as *relocation and protection registers*).

When a program is loaded into memory, it is allocated an amount of space by the supervisor. The starting location in memory and the extent of this space is recorded in the job's data area. When the program is run, the starting location and the extent are loaded into the base and limit registers, respectively. Each memory reference generated by the program, instruction fetch or data fetch, is checked by the hardware to ensure that it lies within the program's area.

Since it is not known where a program will be loaded at the time of compilation, and since a program is not necessarily loaded into the same locations on two separate occasions, it is clear that the addresses generated at the compilation stage cannot be absolute addresses. All addresses in a program which is to run in a multiprogramming mix are such that they are relative to word zero of that program. This means a program cannot be run without some modification to its addresses. The modification required is the addition to each program address of the current starting address of the program. This is the address which is loaded into the base register. The hardware automatically adds (relocates) the contents of the base register to each address generated by the current program. Thus, the function of the base register is to transform relative addresses to absolute addresses.

The purpose of the limit register is to prevent a program accessing memory outside its allocated area. The hardware checks that the relative (i.e., the address generated before the addition of the base register) does not exceed the value in the limit register. If the generated address is less than the value in the limit register, the contents of the base register is added and the memory reference is made. If the limit check fails, than a trap to supervisor is made and the program is suspended. Thus, attempting to reference memory outside the allocated area causes an interrupt. Some machines allow the reading of information from outside the job area, on the basis that this does not corrupt any other information. On some machines, the limit register holds the absolute address of the limit of the job area, in which case the protection check is made after the addition of the base register.

The changing of the contents of the base and limit registers is a privileged operation, which can only be performed by the supervisor. Since the supervisor requires the ability to communicate with all programs in memory, protection need not be applied to addresses generated during running in supervisor mode.

Should a program require more memory during its run, then it issues the appropriate SVC and is suspended until the space becomes available, at which time the supervisor will reset the values of the base and limit registers before running the program.

4.2 Swapping and Time-Slices

In chapter 3, we discussed a number of ways of achieving time-sharing. With a small, simple system, given enough main memory into which to fit all the active users' programs, it would obviously be possible to achieve time-sharing with almost standard multiprogramming techniques. However, even with this simple approach, we should have to take steps to deal with the situation where one of the programs in main memory involved a great deal of computation without any input or output to hold it up. With such a compute-bound job, the other users of the system would suffer a very long response time. It is possible to overcome this by the addition to the hardware of a clock capable of generating an interrupt at regular intervals. Using the clock, it is possible to interrupt a program after a time (its time-slice) and suspend its operation in favour of some other program waiting to run. In this way, each program (user) will get attention from the processor at regular intervals and will not be held up by a long running compute-bound job.

Our simple system, with all active users in main memory at one time, is obviously not feasible for more than a few simultaneous users. However, the principles involved are general, since even in the situation where time-sliced multiprogramming with swapping is being employed, at any given instant the situation in main memory may be regarded as static, and is identical in this way to the simple system just described.

In the previous section, the situation arose where, after servicing an interrupt which released a program from the input/output wait situation, more than one program was in a runnable state. That is, the interrupted job and the job whose input/output operation had just terminated were both runnable. The supervisor must obviously be provided with some mechanism for selecting the next job to be run. Scheduling is discussed in section 5.3 and various scheduling algorithms are examined. No matter which scheduling algorithm is employed to control the total job mix, the relative priorities of all jobs at any instant must be known by the supervisor. In practice, the supervisor may only be interested in knowing which of the jobs in memory has the highest priority. Giving the supervisor this information avoids frequent references to the main scheduling algorithm (program) to resolve such situations as the one above. The priority of jobs in main memory may well be changed dynamically according to the scheduling program, which will be called into operation both at regular intervals of time and on the occurrence of predefined events. Thus, we may regard scheduling as operating at two levels; the scheduling program is operating at the second-by-second level, and beneath this the supervisor is making decisions at the millisecond level. In the previous section, we referred to this part of the supervisor as the selector. We shall continue to use this name to avoid confusion between the scheduler and the selector.

Let us now consider in a little more detail the way the selector works, and at the same time expand a little on the information required by the supervisor for it to accomplish its task. Let us continue for a while with our simple system where all user jobs are in main memory and are being multiprogrammed together, with a clock providing the timing for the time-slices. Basically, there are two types of jobs—those in a runnable state and those waiting for an input/output operation to terminate and therefore not runnable. The supervisor will need two queues—one to deal with the runnable jobs and another to deal with all the suspended jobs—so that when a peripheral terminates the job may be identified. When a peripheral terminates and a job is released, the scheduler must be called to determine this job's position in the runnable job queue. Figure 4.7

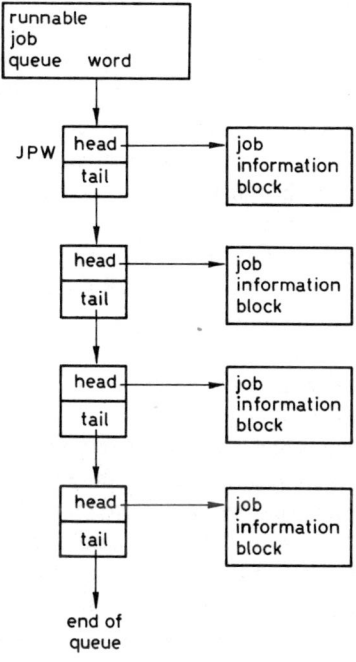

Fig. 4.7

shows a runnable job queue with four jobs in it. The job information block will include such things as the contents of the accumulators and index registers when the job was last suspended, the program counter contents indicating the address within the job of the next instruction to be obeyed, the time-slice allocated to the job (if this is a variable), the total running time allowed for the job together with the time used so far, and other information pertinent to the supervisor. Associated with each job in the queue is a job pointer word (JPW), consisting of a head and a tail. The head points to the job information block for this job and the tail points to the JPW of the job with the next highest priority. The chaining of jobs in this way is carried out by the scheduler. To change priorities, only the tails of the JPWs need be changed.

When a new job is to be selected, the selector picks up the pointer to the JPW of the highest priority job from a standard location, shown in Fig. 4.7, which we shall call the runnable job queue word. Having found the relevant job information block using the head of the JPW, the selector sets the runnable job queue word to be the same as the tail of the JPW of the highest priority job. This removes the top job from the queue and makes the next job down the new highest priority job.

Associated with each peripheral will be a word containing a pointer to the job information block of the job awaiting the termination of the peripheral. When the peripheral terminates, the job becomes runnable and the schedular is called to place the job on the runnable job queue. If the schedular decides to place the job at the top of the queue the following is required. The pointer in the runnable job queue word is placed in the tail of the new job's JPW. This makes the new JPW point to the previous head of the list. The address of the new JPW is placed in the runnable job queue word. Should the schedular decided to place the job at some intermediate point in the queue, it must copy the tail of the JPW of the job above it in the queue to the tail of the new job's JPW and then plant the address of the JPW into the tail of the job above it.

The storage required for maintaining queues is chained together in a free store list. When locations are required for an entry in a queue, the space is acquired from the free store list and subsequently returned when released.

If the system involves swapping programs between main memory and secondary storage, the number of queues administered by the supervisor increases, but the techniques of queue handling remain very much the same. However, a number of complications are introduced by swapping programs, mainly associated with main memory management. Given that there are more jobs to be run than there is main memory to load them into, some jobs will be held on backing store until such times as they can be loaded into memory.

In order to load a job, it is necessary to find sufficient space for it in a contiguous block. A number of solutions are possible. It may be that a job terminates and releases sufficient space to load the job, in which case no problem arises. It may be that between each job loaded in main memory there is a small amount of unused space, which if it were all collected together would be sufficient to load the job. Here, the dilemma is that in order to collect this space together as a contiguous block all jobs must be stopped while the operation takes place.

It is not obvious if this operation is worthwhile or whether it would not be better to give the time over to obeying jobs in the hope that one of them would terminate within a short time, and thus create the required space. If it proves necessary to swap a job out before it has terminated, in order to create space, a number of solutions present themselves. Assuming that the supervisor recognizes two classes of jobs—runnable and non-runnable—then there are two basic choices. We can swap a non-runnable job on the basis that it is held up anyway. However, this presents problems, in that if the input/output operation for which the job has been suspended is actually in progress, the buffer area into or out of which the transfer is taking place may suddenly disappear with obvious disastrous results. If the input/output operation has not taken place, then swapping the job out places a burden on the supervisor in that it must create a buffer area for the transfer and manage this buffer until such time as the job returns when the contents of the buffer must be passed to the job. The other choice is to swap a runnable job, say the one on the end of the runnable job queue, which is likely to be the most recently run which did not get suspended for input/output. This choice presents no major problems and is the obvious solution.

The swapping of jobs can be approached in two ways. Assuming that there are jobs in a runnable state on the swapping device, then we may force a swap to take place, either when the scheduler decides that a non-resident job should be run or whenever a job terminates its run. In the first instance, the basic philosophy is to swap only as a last resort, and in the latter case it is to swap a job as soon as it is suspended at the end of its time-slice (but not for input/output) so as to give processor time to those not in main memory. In this latter case, the runnable job queue may be considered as all the runnable jobs; those at the front of the queue are in main memory and those at the back are on the swapping device.

There is a further problem concerned with making main memory space available. If a job is swapped out, it may not create sufficient space for the job waiting to be swapped in. In this case, either we may choose to swap in some other job that will fit into the available space or we may swap out more jobs until enough space is created. Ultimately, we may *have* to keep swapping jobs to create sufficient space for a large job. If the scheduler chooses to by-pass a large job at any stage, the next time an attempt is made to load the job the likelihood of it being loaded should be increased. A further solution to this problem is to try and select a job to swap out which is large enough to create sufficient space. This would obviously involve the supervisor in maintaining further information which identifies jobs by the amount of space they occupy. Since jobs dynamically change their demands on main memory, this is not quite as simple as it sounds. With such a scheme, this table would also have to identify the status (runnable or non-runnable) of jobs to avoid selecting a job held up for input/output.

On a simple system, the time-slice would be the same for all jobs. However, with a more complex scheduling algorithm, variable-length time-slices would be allocated. The time-slice might be a function of such things as the size of the job (which itself varies dynamically), and the elapsed time since the last run. Large jobs would be run (and therefore swapped) less frequently to avoid excess pressure on the swapping channel, but given longer time-slices to compensate for this. A job that for some reason had not been run for some time (it might have been swapped out) might be given a larger than normal time-slice for its next run to make up for this.

In this section we have described some of the problems to be overcome in order to achieve time-sharing involving program swapping. In order to make the explanation easier, we have simplified a number of things. In particular, we have only considered the supervisor handling two queues, but on a typical system there may be many queues to administer. Nevertheless, the principles remain true.

4.3 Paging and Segmentation

Memory mapping. In the previous section, we noted that one of the problems associated with program swapping is the management of main memory. When a program has to be swapped in, the problem is to find or create a sufficiently large contiguous area to hold it. With a number of programs in main memory, the free areas become scattered and occur at program boundaries, with the result that the main memory is not fully utilized. One solution to this problem is to introduce a mapping mechanism between the address generated by the central processor and the main memory address. Such a mapping mechanism (discussed above in section 3.5) is shown in Figs 4.8 and 4.9. Main memory is partitioned into fixed-length blocks or page frames. The program and the data are conceptually partitioned into pages of the same size as the blocks. This partitioning would be transparent to the user. Any address computed by the CPU is partitioned into page number and line number.

Suppose the block size (and therefore the page size) is 512 words, and the computed address occupies eighteen bits. The upper nine bits would be taken as the page number and the lower nine bits as the line or displacement with the page. The page number p is used by the hardware to access the pth register in the map. (The map as shown in Figs 4.8 and 4.9 consists of a group of registers, one for each page frame of physical main memory.) The contents of this register are

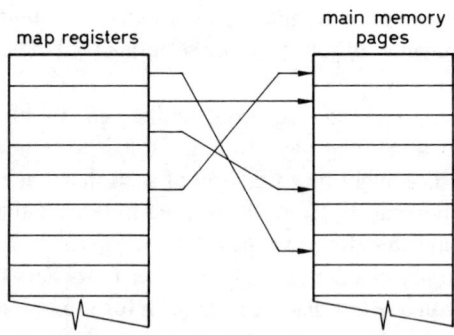

Fig. 4.8

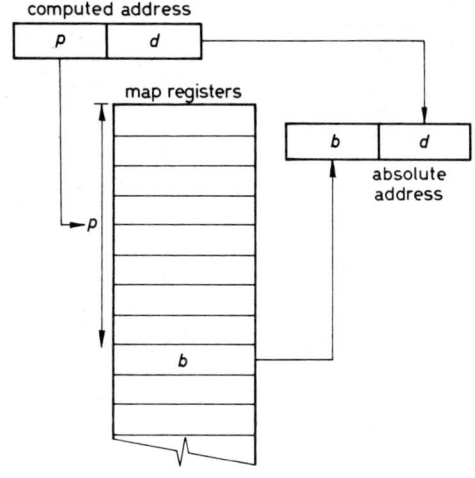

Fig. 4.9

the starting address of the page frame in main memory holding this page. The starting address obtained from the map is combined with the line number to form the correct main memory address. This is shown in Fig. 4.9.

With the system described above, it is possible to allocate any free blocks to a program. The blocks need not be contiguous since the contents of a map register is independant of its position. The advantage of such a mapping mechanism is that the management of main memory becomes much simpler, the allocation unit being of fixed length and there being no need to find contiguous blocks to hold a program.

Since in a swapping system programs may be loaded in different parts of main memory on a number of occasions, the contents of that part of the map relating to a given job must be set up at the time of loading that job. Moreover, since the computed addresses are not affected by the position of the program in main memory, the page numbers generated by the processor will always be the same for a given program. Thus, the registers (not their contents) within the map used by a given program are fixed. Those map registers used by a job must therefore be treated in a similar fashion to the index and general-purpose registers and their contents must be preserved within the job's information area whenever the job is suspended. Similarly, when the job is rerun the relevant part of the map is reinstated from the job information area, together with the other registers. (This saved and restored information is collectively called the job's 'state word'.) Since a job may address only main memory using that part of the map allocated to it, main memory not allocated to the job is protected.

During the course of, say, editing, compiling, and executing a program, the user's main memory area, and therefore his use of the map, will grow and

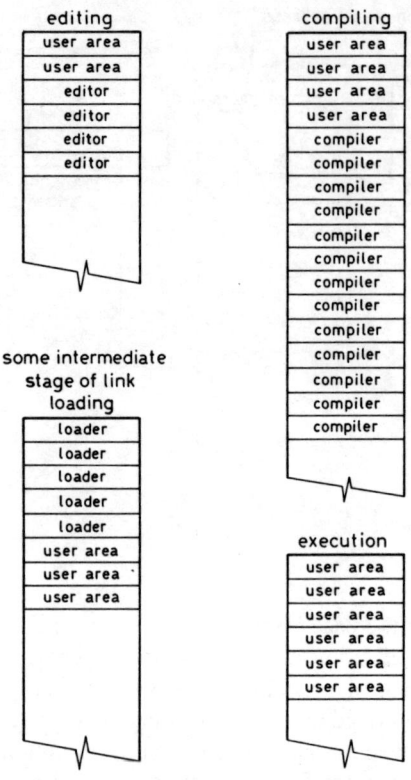

Fig. 4.10

contract dynamically, reflecting the user's action and demands upon the system at any stage. Fig. 4.10 shows the contents of the map at various stages for some typical job. This constant changing of main memory requirements is considerably simplified with a map, since, when a job is demanding more memory, areas required need not be contiguous and, when contracting, released memory becomes immediately available to other users irrespective of its position.

We mentioned earlier that the supervisor (in general, any program executed in supervisor mode, which will include all or most of the operating system) has certain privileges over user mode programs. One such privilege is to address all the main memory. This is accomplished by executing supervisor mode instructions independently of the mapping mechanism. It is clear that the application of the mapping mechanism adds time to the instruction cycle. In executing an instruction, there is one memory reference to fetch the instruction and then, typically, a memory reference to read or write data. In the discussions above, we have assumed that all memory references in user mode are mapped. However, considerable time can be saved if the memory reference to fetch the instruction is not mapped. The program counter register is initially set up to point to the absolute address of the first word of the program, and changed whenever a page boundary is crossed or when a jump instruction is executed. Instructions are directly fetched from memory, using only the program counter register, but the data address within the instruction is mapped. In order to make the logic of the machine simpler, the contents of the program counter register is recalculated (using the map) at each jump, whether or not this causes a page change.

Paging. We have emphasized that the success of multiprogramming depends upon there being sufficient jobs in main memory to ensure that the supervisor is always able to find a runnable job. Jobs which demand a large amount of main memory obviously mitigated against this ideal situation. In particular, any installation running with mainly large jobs (relative to the size of main memory) will find it difficult to utilize multiprogramming techniques fully where all parts of a job have to be in main memory at run time. One solution to this problem is to break the program into pages as before, but only load into main memory a few of the total number of pages at any given instant. This requires that there is a mechanism for detecting that a generated address relates to a page not loaded, thus causing an interrupt to supervisor to fetch this page. As in the case of the memory map, the computed address is regarded as being made up of page number and displacement within the page. Each job in the system has associated with it a page table showing at any given instant the distribution of the pages of the job between main memory and the swapping device(s). When a given job is running, its page table is loaded into main memory and a register in the CPU is loaded to point to the base and limit of the page table. The most significant bits of the computed address are used as an index into the page table (using the contents of the page table register as a base and a check). The entry obtained from the page table will be either the starting address in main memory of the page, or an indication that the page is not in main memory (the left-hand bit of the word, say), in which case the contents of the entry is treated as an address on the swapping device. This is shown in Fig. 4.11. If the page is in main memory, the address obtained from the page table is combined with the low-order bits of the computed address to form the absolute address in main memory in much the same way as with the memory map. If the page is not in memory, the hardware generates an SVC to cause the page to be loaded by the supervisor. In this case, the job is suspended, the state word (which includes the page table register) is stored and the state word of the next job to run is set up. Thus, the transfer of the required page is overlapped with computations being performed by other jobs, using standard multiprogramming techniques.

The paging technique described above (and in chapter 3) has the disadvantage that each instruction takes an extra main memory cycle to reference the page table. It would be normal, as in the case of the memory map, to treat the program counter separately in order to avoid yet another memory reference. It is possible, at the expense of more complicated hardware, to avoid most extra memory references in paging by using an associative look up for each generated

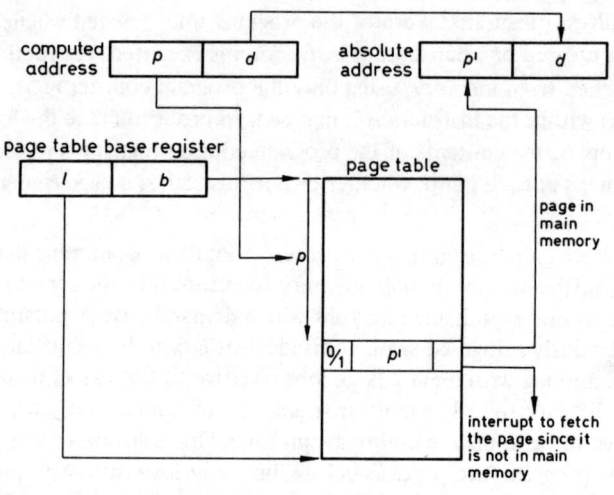

Fig. 4.11

address. Fast associative registers are used to hold the generated page numbers and the associated starting addresses in main memory of the most recently accessed pages of the current job. Typically, there might be eight such registers. The first action of the hardware is to take the most significant bits of the computed address and compare them simultaneously with the corresponding bits in each of the associative registers. If a match is found, the starting address held in the register is used with the low-order bits of the computed address to obtain the absolute address. If no match is found, then the page table is indexed as before. When the page has been fetched, an associative register is updated to contain a reference to this new page. This is illustrated in Fig. 4.12. Provided that at any given period of activity of a job a small number of pages are in use, the provision of associative registers avoids extra memory references in most instructions.

One great advantage of paging is that there is no reason why the job should not be larger than the physical main memory, since at no point in time are all the pages of a job required to be present in main memory. This fact is often catered for by allowing the programmer to address space greater than physical main memory. This gives rise to the term 'virtual memory'. Thus, for example, it is possible to give a programmer a 24 bit address field which might be split into 14 bits for the page number and 10 bits for the displacement. This gives an address space of $16K$ pages, each of $1K$ words, a total of $16M$ words. This obviously bears no relationship to physical memory. There are problems in creating such a large address space, in that the page table is $16K$ words long and will itself be paged and swapped in and out. The advantage of a virtual memory is that programs larger than main memory do not have to be overlayed, thus removing the attendant problems and work which the programmer has to undertake if overlaying techniques are used. However, with a system running only small jobs, paging does not appear to be such an attractive proposition.

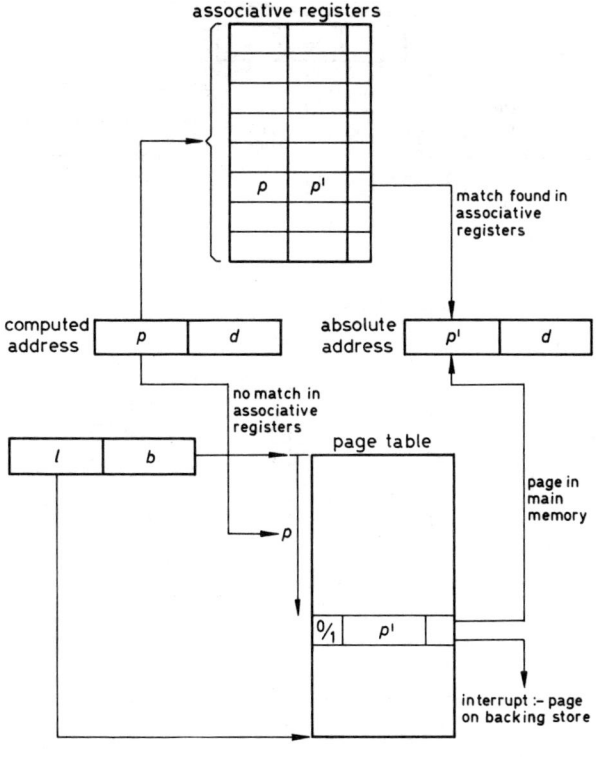

Fig. 4.12

Segmentation. Segmentation is a scheme whereby each section of a job such as the main program, subroutines, and data areas is addressed separately. This is by no means a new concept, but on earlier generation machines it was usual to allocate a fixed amount of memory to each segment at the time the segment was first loaded into memory. Thus, the programmer had to ensure that sufficient space was requested by each segment in order to allow it to grow as the execution progressed. This is particularly critical in the case of data areas and work space, in that these are the areas that grow and contract unpredictably. In some instances, it is difficult, if not impossible, to predict the amount of space required by a particular segment in advance. In such a case, what is required is that the space allocation be determined at run time. To accomplish this, the computed address is split into three parts—segment number, page number, and displacement. Each job in the system has associated with it a segment table. The segment table register is set to point to the base and limit of the current user's segment table. The segment number is used to index into the segment table. The entry obtained from the segment table gives the base and limit of the page table for that segment. The page number is used as an index into this page table to

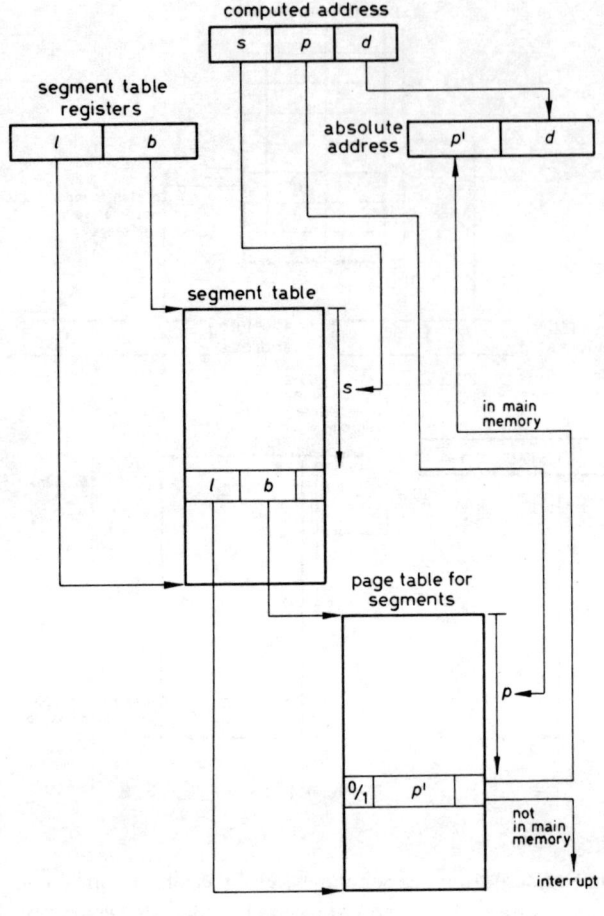

Fig. 4.13

obtain the starting address in main memory (or otherwise) of the page, to which is added the displacement.

The process of generating an obsolute address is shown in Fig. 4.13. Such a scheme involves three memory cycles to access a word, and is obviously not viable as such. Once again, a set of associative registers is used to ensure that the majority of words can be accessed in a single cycle together with a lookup in the associative registers. In this case, the entries in the associative registers consist of segment number-page number pairs. The scan is made using the s and p of the computed address. If a match is found, the associative register yields the starting address in main memory of the required page. If a match is not found, then three memory cycles are required. As before, the associative registers are kept up to date to reflect the pages currently in use by the job. The associative registers and the segment table register form part of the state word of the job.

Suppose the computed address is 40 bits long, and that the segment number occupies 12 bits, the page number 18 bits, and displacement 10 bits. Thus, each user has access to a virtual memory consisting of $4K$ segments each of $256M$ words; so each segment is sufficiently large to allow expansion at run time. It should be noted that each user has a unique segment table, but that if a number of users are using the same segment there need only be one page table for this segment and it will be pointed to by each of the segment tables using it. In the MULTICS system, files and segments are synonymous and thus segmentation also forms the basis of file sharing.

It is possible to avoid swapping out pages which have not changed since they were brought into main memory by associating a bit with each page which is changed the first time the page is written to. When the page frame is required for an incoming page, this bit is checked by hardware. If the contents have not changed then an exact copy will exist on the swapping device, so that there is no need to swap this page out and it can be overwritten, thereby reducing the traffic on the swapping channel.

If two bits (or more) are associated with each entry in a page or segment table then the pages or segments may be protected. For example, with two bits one is able to make a segment available for reading only, reading and writing, and execution only. If a segment is being shared by a number of users, it is possible that the owner of the segment may wish to prevent other users from writing to (and therefore destroying or changing) the segment, at the same time retaining this privilege himself. This is possible because each user has a unique segment table, and the protection bits may be set differently on each segment table for the same segment.

Paging and segmentation give rise to a number of problems. These can be summarized briefly as follows:

(a) Choosing the page size. It is important that an optimum page size is chosen (this particular point applies to memory mapping as well as paging). If it is too large, much available space could be wasted within pages. If it is too small, the system overheads associated with the management of the paging system could well become excessive. A further conflict arises in that the requirement of executable code is for a large page size so that it may run uninterrupted for long periods, whereas associated with any program are a number of small data areas for which a smaller page size would be more appropriate. Examples of page sizes currently in use are now cited in order to give an appreciation of the wide variability in the choice of page sizes: the XDS Sigma 7 (which employs a mapping system) usues a page size of 512 words, as do the larger machines in the ICL range. The IBM 360/67 uses a page size of 4096 bytes, whereas the MULTICS project utilizing a GE 645 has two page sizes, 1024 and 64 words. At the other end of the scale, the Burroughs B5000 utilizes a variable page size (up to a maximum of 1024 words), depending upon an automatic allocation request determined at compile time. The conclusion, therefore, is that there is no general

rule which can be applied in determining an optimum page size, as it is very much experimental as well as machine-dependent.

(b) Page replacement. It is necessary to make room in memory for new information (i.e., a new page for a program currently loaded or the first page of a new program) and this will necessitate swapping out a page or overwriting a page which has been unaltered while resident. In the latter case, this means introducing into the system a marker within the page table, to indicate whether a particular page in memory has been unaltered (not written to) and therefore does not have to be copied onto backing store. In the former case (i.e., swapping a page), an effective algorithm has to be determined for deciding which page should be swapped out. This can be a difficult process and various techniques are used. For example, we may choose to swap out the page that has been longest in memory or, more elaborately, the least-accessed page which has been longest in memory. Algorithms of a much more sophisticated nature based on a 'learning' process and the past history of all the resident pages can be constructed. A typical example of this type of approach is found in the ICL Atlas computer. The algorithm in this case attempts to find a page no longer in use and, if it is unable to find such a page, attempts, on the basis of the recent pattern of activity, to locate a page which will not be used for the longest time. Again, as with the choice of page size, algorithms for page replacement are still experimental and the degree of sophistication has to be weighed against the increase in system overheads.

(c) Page fetching.—As we have seen earlier, a page fetch will be initiated when the active program references a page not currently in memory. There are a number of algorithms concerning page fetching, the simplest of which is termed *demand paging* and consists of fetching only the required page. Other, more elaborate algorithms attempt to predict which other pages may be required in the near future and brings these in as well. Although paging aims to reduce data flow and improve main memory utilization, the speed of the swapping device can still be critical if the job mix and/or the available memory is such that the system cannot guarantee the availability of another executable program while swapping takes place. However, since paging means that more user tasks will be resident for a given amount of main memory, the speed of the swapping device may not be quite as critical as in some of the previous methods of achieving time-sharing.

4.4 Re-entrant coding

Let us consider a $32K$ system where the operating system requires $12K$, thus leaving $20K$ for the users. Suppose that, over a short period of time, there are 16 users logged on to the system. Of these 16, let us suppose that 9 are creating files using an editor, 3 are compiling FORTRAN programs, 2 are compiling BASIC programs, and 2 are manipulating files. Let us assume that the editor occupies $2K$, $1K$ for the package and $1K$ for the user, the FORTRAN compiler requires

10K plus an average of 1K for each user, BASIC requires 6K plus 1K per user, and the file manipulation package occupies 1K, which includes user space. Thus, the total memory required is:

$$9 \times 2 + 3 \times 11 + 2 \times 7 + 2 \times 1 = 67K$$

Since only 20K is available to the users, at least 47K must be swapped out at any given instant in the period of time under consideration. Now, suppose that, instead of each user using a separate copy of any given system program, only a single copy of the relevant programs is required. In this case, the total space required is:

$$(1 + 9 \times 1) + (10 + 3 \times 1) + (6 + 2 \times 1) + (2 \times 1) = 33K$$

Thus, main memory space is exceeded by only 13K. It is clear that the response time will be considerably better (for the 16 users in this case) with such an arrangement, since there is less information requiring to be swapped.

In order to achieve sharing of code, it is necessary that the shared code does not change as a result of being obeyed. What this really implies is not so much that the code itself should not change (in general, it would be unusual for the *code* to change) but that the workspace used should be separate from the sharable code. This workspace includes such things as locations used to hold intermediate data, links to internal subroutines, and, of course, the machine registers. The solution is to make these workspace locations lie within the user's area. Thus, if two users are sharing a section of code there will be two copies of the workspace—one for each user. When the first user is running, the shared code is referencing workspace within that user's area. When the second is running, the shared code accesses the workspace in this user's area. In this way, a number of users may share code without interfering with each other. The names commonly applied to sharable code are 're-entrant' or 'pure' code.

One result of using re-entrant code for systems programs is that since re-entrant code does not change they need never be swapped out because an exact copy will exist on the swapping device from the time it was first swapped in. Since swapping is one of the critical areas of a time-sharing system, and since systems programs tend to be large and therefore take a long time to swap, this is a considerable advantage. It should be noted that in the case of a roll-in/roll-out system this is the major advantage gained from re-entrant code, since each user is loaded independently of the other users and no main memory saving is affected.

Although the concept of sharing code is simple enough, there are a few problems which have to be solved in order to maintain the integrity of the system. Consider a machine with a base-limit register which is used by the hardware to restrict the area of memory which a user may access at any given instant. If access outside the user's allocated area is prohibited then sharing code in another part of memory is not possible.

One solution to this problem is to arrange to run re-entrant code in supervisor mode. Since in this mode no address relocation and bound checking takes place, the re-entrant code is able to access the user's area. It would be a function of the operating system to set up the necessary links between the re-entrant code and the particular user program. The disadvantage of such an approach is the amount of main memory space required if the allocation of main memory within the operating system area is permanent. With a permanent allocation within the operating system area, it would be possible to use this area for any re-entrant system software that would fit into the space, but would probably mean that only one compiler at a time could be in memory. It would probably also mean that, even with no compiler in memory, this space would not be available to users.

Another solution to this problem is to introduce the concept of a 'trusted' program. Such a program would be treated in some respects like a user program and in others like a program running in supervisor mode. It would be loaded into the general users' memory area and swapped and relocated like a user program but would not have a limit register check applied (alternatively, the limit register could be loaded with a value such that any address generated by the trusted program would appear to be valid). The operating system would, as before, have to set up the linkage between the compiler and the user program. Such a compiler (or other system software) must be as error-free as possible before one would trust it to run in this mode, since the integrity of the system depends on it.

A far better solution is to provide a second base-limit register. One base-limit register is used to relocate and protect the user program and the second is used to relocate and protect the re-entrant code. The problem in this case is to determine which register is to be applied to a particular address. One approach is to use the most significant bit of the address field to indicate which base-limit register to use. This has the effect of halving the address space available to the user, and obviously this solution is not feasible on a machine which has a restricted address space. Addresses generated within the re-entrant code which reference workspace would have the most significant bit of the address field zero (say). This would cause these addresses to be relocated and checked using the current user's base-limit register. Those references internal to the re-entrant code, such as the address of the next instruction and addresses of constants would have the most significant address bit set to one and would be relocated and checked using the base-limit register for the re-entrant code. Another way of using two base-limit registers is to use one to relocate/protect the program counter (the re-entrant code) and the second to relocate/protect the operand addresses.

Let us consider the problem of sharing code when operating with a memory map. If a user wishes to use a compiler, say, then, assuming there is a copy in main memory, all that is required of the operating system is to include the page addresses of the compiler in the user's copy of the map registers. In this way, the compiler becomes available to that user. It becomes necessary, however, to ensure that the pages occupied by the compiler are protected in such a way that the user is unable to change their contents. Also, if a number of users are sharing a single copy of a compiler then a problem arises when it comes to swapping. Suppose, for example, that there are three users sharing the BASIC compiler. If one of the jobs is swapped out then it is clear that the compiler must not be swapped (overwritten), since this would prevent the other two jobs from running. The compiler must be held in main memory until such time as all jobs have ceased to use it. If at any stage all the jobs using the BASIC compiler are swapped out of main memory, then there would seem to be a case for releasing the memory space occupied by the compiler. However, if the compiler is overwritten then when the jobs using the compiler and the compiler itself are returned to main memory, all copies of the map registers for the jobs using the compiler will have to be updated to reflect the new position of the pages of the compiler, since it is unlikely that the compiler will return to the same position in memory. This overhead on the operating system must be weighed against the effect of releasing the memory occupied by the compiler.

With paging, if one regards the page table as a map of the user's virtual memory, then the situation is the same as in the case of a memory map.

With segmentation, all that is required is to make an entry in the segment tables of each user requiring the compiler. Each segment table entry will point to the same page table, namely that page table relating to the compiler. Thus, the system automatically keeps track of the compiler through its unique page table (unlike the memory map and demand paging, where each user's map had to be updated if the compiler or part of it moved). The ease with which code may be shared is one of the main arguments in favour of segmentation.

In summary, in all cases except perhaps in the case of a roll-in/roll-out system, there are immense advantages to be gained using re-entrant code in terms of saving main memory space and in terms of reducing the load on the swapping channel. These two items are the prime factors which determine the success or otherwise of a time-sharing system.

4.5 Compilers and Interpreters

There are two basic forms of translation process used to convert statements written in a programming language into executable machine code. The most common of these processes uses a compiler. Here, the source code is transformed by the compiler into an executable machine code program which is logically equivalent to the original source program. The compilation process may involve a single scan of the source code, resulting directly in the object code. Such a compiler is termed a 'single-pass' compiler. In other cases, one or more intermediate phases are involved which may include the production of code in yet another language. Such compilers are termed 'multipass'. Often, a subsequent pass is included in order to optimize the code produced by an earlier pass. Finally, on systems which allow programs to be written in more than one language, and then combined by the linking loader, the code produced by all compilers will need processing by the leader to produce executable machine-code. Thus, we see that even with compilers there are a number of approaches.

The important aspects of a compiler are its speed of compilation, the efficiency of the code it produces in terms of both speed and space, the size of the compiler itself, the compile-time and run-time diagnostics, and the type of code produced. This latter point is of importance to professional programmers familiar with assembly code programming since, if dynamic debugging is provided in assembly or machine code, the programmer may choose to debug, say, a difficult FORTRAN program in its object code form rather than its source code form. In this case, it is essential that the object program can easily be related to the source program.

Obviously, object code debugging is far from ideal, but few systems offer dynamic debugging in source code for high-level languages such as FORTRAN or BASIC. The basic requirements of dynamic debugging are the ability to stop a program at some intermediate point, to examine the values of variables and program locations, to change the value of variables, and to change, delete, and insert source code. It is fairly straightforward to provide break-point facilities and allow access to the symbol table to print the value of variables. The main difficulty is to allow the program to be changed in source code, since the translation to object code involves the compiler.

One solution to the problem is to provide an incremental compiler. Such a compiler is a single-pass compiler which produces object code for each statement as it is typed. The object code produced is modular, and each block of code (corresponding to a single statement) is linked to the next block by a standard linking mechanism. At run time, it is possible to stop a program, present a new statement to the compiler, and have it 'patched in' at the appropriate point by changing the links of the adjacent modules of object code. One by-product of such a compiler is that the sequence of presenting the statements of the program to the compiler is immaterial. Another is that the user is notified of syntax errors as soon as they are detected on a line-by-line basis. An incremental compiler is ideal for the language BASIC. An example of a dialog which might take place using an incremental compiler for BASIC is given below.

```
NEW HISTOGRAM
READY

5 REM TO DRAW A HISTOGRAM
10 READ N
20 FOR I=1 TO N
30 READ A[I],F[I]
40 NEXT
ERROR--CONTROLLED VARIABLE MISSING
                        Error detected retype the line
40 NEXT I
50 PRINT
60 PRINT A[I];
55 FOR I=1 TO N          insert a line
70 FOR J=1 TO F[I]
```

```
80 PRINT "-";
90 NEXT J
100 NEXT I
200 DATA 8
210 DATA 1,2,2,4,3,10,4,12,5,15,6,12,7,5,8,1
220 END
RUN

HISTOGRAM      28-5-70

1--2----3---                    stop the program there's something
                                wrong.
HALTED AT LINE 80               we stopped in the middle of 80
58 PRINT                        insert line to correct program
CONTINUE                        and continue from middle of 80!
-----;
4------------
5---------------
6--------
7-----
8-                              seems to be working
END OF PROGRAM
RUN                             but check it again in full

HISTOGRAM      28-5-70

1--
2----
3----------
4------------
5---------------
6------------
7-----
8-                              correct!
END OF PROGRAM
```

    The major disadvantages of this method are that the run-time efficiency is poor, since it is of necessity a single-pass compiler and there is an overhead in linking the modules together, and that the main memory space–time product is high, since the compiler is required all the time the program is being typed in.

    An alternative method, which provides dynamic debugging facilities, is interpreting. In the case of a compiler, object code is produced and executed independently of the compiler. In the case of an interpreter, each line of source code is translated and executed immediately—no object code is produced, all execution being accomplished by entering standard subroutines with appropriate parameters and then returning control to the interpreter. This means that each statement, even if it appears within a loop, is translated and executed each time it is met, thus the interpreter is an integral part of the executing process. Since the code is scanned afresh each time, if an editing facility is provided to delete, insert, and change lines of the program, dynamic debugging is automatically provided. Almost all implementations of JOSS (or its derivatives) are interpreters.

The drawbacks of interpreters are that execution is very slow (compared with executing the equivalent compiled code), and since the interpreter, which tends to be large, is present while the program is being typed in (checking the syntax) and at execution time, the main memory space–time product is high. The advantage is the range of dynamic debugging facilities which it is possible to provide.

The main disadvantage of providing dynamic debugging facilities is that the run-time efficiency is often poor. In debugging a program this is of no consequence, but if the program becomes a production program then this efficiency may well be critical. The ideal solution is to have dynamic debugging facilities plus a compatible optimizing compiler for use once the program has been debugged and is required for production work. Unfortunately, ideals are hard to find!

4.6 System Architecture

In considering a system, one must evaluate both the software and the hardware. The evaluation of the software involves such things as analysing the code produced by compilers, comparing the size of similar compilers and other software items, and comparing the diagnostic and debugging aids provided with each language. The evaluation of the hardware is in some senses more difficult, since the various aspects of system architecture interact with one another. In many cases, bad system architecture will manifest itself in the software evaluation. Poor architecture often causes large compilers, poor object code, and operating systems which are large in proportion to their power and sophistication. We may consider system architecture under three broad headings.

Instruction set. The design of the instruction set may be considered from three viewpoints, two of which are in some ways similar. Firstly, one must look at the available instructions from the viewpoint of the supervisor (and operating system) writer. In this case, one is concerned with instructions which will ensure efficiency in the supervisor. Since it is likely that on entry into supervisor the general-purpose registers will have to be preserved and restored on exit, it is necessary that this be a fast simple operation. Some machines have two instructions which accomplish these tasks directly—an obvious advantage over machines which need a number of time- and space-consuming instructions to accomplish the same result. If items such as the priority of routines under control of the supervisor are held as a bit list in a word, then the supervisor is faced with the problem of scanning such a bit list in order to find the most significant one. Some machines are able to scan such a word and generate in a single instruction a number indicating the position within the word of the most significant one. In a word machine, the handling of characters is most important and on some machines no explicit provision is made for this type of operation. A word machine with special character-handling instructions will most probably be more efficient (in terms of time and space) than one without.

Secondly, one must look at the instruction set from the point of view of the compiler writer. One frequent requirement is to create a push-down stack (or first-in-last-out list). Some machines have instructions for administering stacks in memory (adding new items and deleting existing items). Such instructions offer an enormous advantage to the compiler writer. In a recursive language such as ALGOL, stack techniques are employed to implement recursion. Another requirement for dealing with recursion is multilevel subroutine nesting. This nesting should not require a register and should be fast. Since on the first scan the source code is being handled at the character level, good character handling facilities are required.

In order to produce efficient code, the compiler writer needs a full and rich instruction set. Thus, one should look for such things as: register-to-register operations; routing of results to memory and/or registers; a full set of conditional instructions of both the skip and jump variety; and a full set of logical and bit testing instructions.

Finally, one must look at the instruction set from the point of view of the user. If the above two categories are well catered for, it follows that the general user facilities will be more than adequate. However, over and above the requirements of the system programmers, a user requires good floating-point instructions.

Operational design. There are a number of desirable features concerned with the instruction format. There is an advantage if the hardware allows for immediate operands in all or most instructions where it is appropriate. This saves space, in that the operand appears within the instruction word rather than in a separate word. It also saves time, since there is no memory reference to fetch the operand. Another desirable feature is multilevel indirect addressing. Examples of the use of indirect addressing are for passing parameters to a subroutine by reference, for exiting from a subroutine, and for handling linked lists. It is desirable for complete generality and flexibility that indexing should be possible at each level of indirection. A large address field has a number of advantages. Firstly, large physical main memories may be addressed directly without recourse to base addressing (often the base address has to be handled by the programmer, thus making the machine more difficult and tedious to use). Secondly, a large address field allows large immediate operands. The more general-purpose registers available to the programmer, the more efficient is the code. There is an advantage to be gained if the registers available to the user are truly general purpose. That is, each is usable as an accumulator, an index register, or a memory location. This latter case implies that both program and data may be stored in registers at the user's wish. Executing a program in the registers will be faster than in main memory, since the access time will be much faster for the registers. (This can be very useful to shorten critical paths through the supervisor, particularly when the machine is run with interrupts inhibited, since this time should be kept to an absolute minimum.)

Input/output. In this case, we are concerned with all peripherals on a machine. When comparing the fast peripheral devices on two machines, one must look not only at their latency and transfer rates, but also at the way in which they are interfaced to the machine. In particular, one must consider the interference caused to the CPU by a fast device accessing main memory. Thus, for example, on a machine which has a single access path to memory, shared by the CPU and all fast devices, the throughput on the system will be below that of a machine of similar speed with two paths to memory. On a dual (or more) path system it is possible for a channel serving a fast device to be accessing one block of memory while the processor is accessing a second block through the second path. This is shown in Fig. 4.14. With only a single path, the processor is delayed while the device steals memory cycles. The more fast devices there are, the more acute the problem becomes. Ideally, each fast channel requires its own path to memory.

Assuming that the slow peripherals are on a single multiplexer channel, one must measure and compare the interference to the CPU caused by an 'average' and maximum loading of this channel.

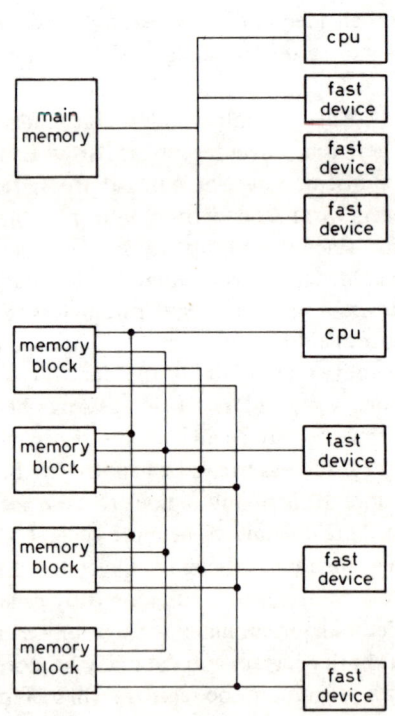

Fig. 4.14 *(a)* Single path to main memory; *(b)* four paths to main memory

Obviously, in a time-sharing system, an area of critical importance is the communication subsystem. The load that this part puts upon the CPU should be measured and compared, particularly in the case of hardware multiplexers and communication processors which pass only a single character at a time across to the main memory. The way faster terminals (e.g., remote batch terminals) are handled is more critical than the way Teletypes, say, are handled.

4.7 Multiplexers and Communication Processors

Multiplexers. A multiplexer is a scanning mechanism which controls the transmission and reception of data between a central processor and a number of data terminals. The typical action of a multiplexer is shown in Fig. 4.15. It is clear that the time t must be such that no characters are 'lost' owing to a line not being serviced in time. In practice, Fig. 4.15 represents a much simplified picture, particularly when the multiplexer has a common memory system for each line, rather than a single character buffer for each line. The methods of line scanning will be dealt with later.

We can divide multiplexers into two main classes.

(a) Hardware multiplexers. These exhibit a number of characteristics.
  (i) They have a limited 'instruction set' which enables them to accomplish the task required of them.
  (ii) A duplication of hardware to detect and assemble characters and to synchronize the character sampling is required for each line (in the asynchronous case).

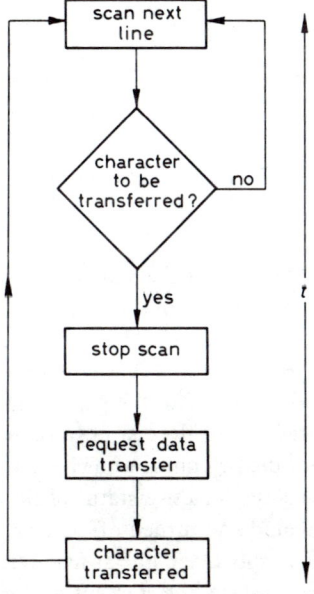

Fig. 4.15

(iii) The speed of the line associated with any given port is fixed by the 'program' wired into the multiplexer.

(iv) There may be a duplication of character buffers for each line.

(b) Those which make use of a communication processor. These exhibit the following characteristics.

(i) They have an instruction set which enables a more flexible approach to be taken to the data communication problem, e.g., data checking.

(ii) The processor can carry out the line scanning by software. This demands a fast processor but saves on the cost of the individual line interfaces.

(iii) The speed of the line serviced may be changed under program control.

(iv) The characters are assembled into the memory of the communication processor, eliminating the need for character buffers.

Let us now look in some detail at the characteristics of asynchronous and synchronous line interfaces.

Asynchronous line interfaces. The characters presented to the interface consist of a series of electrical pulses with two voltage levels used to represent zero and one. A character waveform is shown in Fig. 4.16. The beginning of the character is

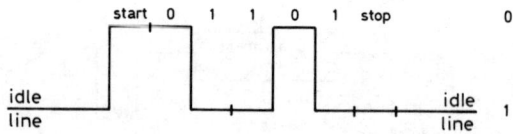

Fig. 4.16 Line state for the five-bit character 01101

clearly defined by the leading edge of the start pulse. Using this as a reference, the interface must synchronize so that it samples each bit of the character in the middle, to minimize any chance of error. Once the beginning of a character has been detected, the end of the character is easily determined by counting the number of bits sampled (consistent with the particular character code) or by detecting the start bit shifted out of the last position in the character assembly buffer (see later). To detect the beginning of a character, the interface requires a flip-flop which records the active/inactive status of the line. The flip-flop gets set when the start pulse is detected and turned off when a complete character has been received. If the flip-flop shows the line as inactive, and the data line goes from the one-state to the zero-state, the start bit of the incoming character is indicated.

There are two methods which can be used to sample the middle of each bit.

(a) A clock which has a start-up time equal to one-half a bit time, and whose frequency equals the bit rate of the line being sampled.

(b) A counter which causes a sample to be taken when it overflows.

The clock is seldom used because of the inherent variation of such a low-speed clock, which would cause it to drift from the centre of each bit. The counter, in order to overcome the same problem, is driven by a high-speed clock which has a rate n times that of the bit rate. By taking the sample on overflow from the counter, we shall more acurately sample the centre of each bit.

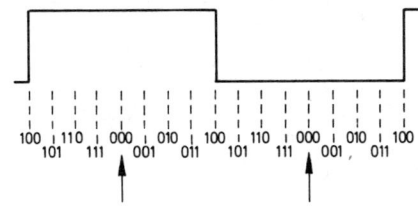

Fig. 4.17 Sampling using three-bit counter and overflow

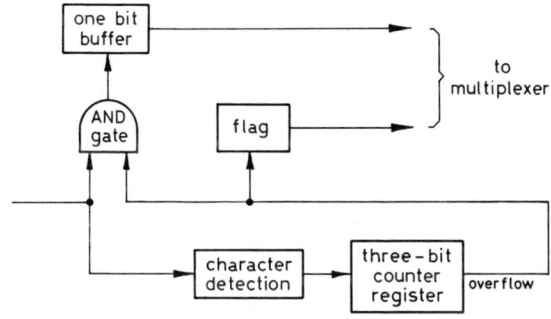

Fig. 4.18 Asynchronous line interface logic

A common sampling design uses a three-bit counter (a count of eight) that gets set to four when the leading edge of the start pulse is detected. The counter is incremented at eight times the bit rate, using overflow to generate a sample. This is shown in Fig. 4.17. The interface logic is shown in Fig. 4.18 and the flow-chart of the action of such an interface is shown in Fig. 4.19.

In designing an interface for handling a few lines (say less than six), a duplication of the complete interface logic for each line is sufficient. However, if all the lines are the same speed, the clock can be made common to all lines. With an increase in the number of lines, a significant cost saving can be realized by eliminating as much redundancy as possible.

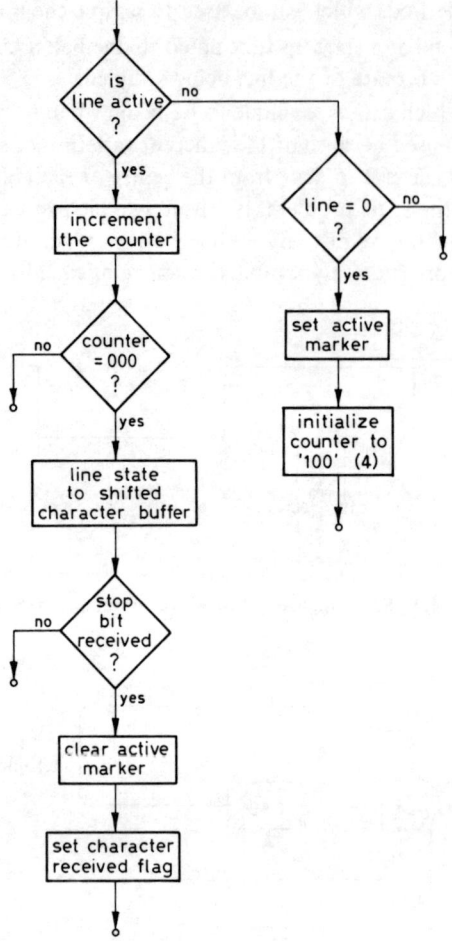

Fig. 4.19

One of the first steps taken to reduce the cost of a serial line interface is to eliminate the received character buffer and assemble into a memory common to all lines. Two such common memories are delay lines and core memory. Core memory is more expensive than delay lines, but its higher-speed and random-access characteristics make it useful for handling many lines and for mixing the line speeds.

Start bit detection, sample synchronization, and character assembly detection must remain as hardware unique to each line. A typical common memory system is shown in Fig. 4.20. The line interface for such a system is shown in Fig. 4.21.

With the introduction of a communication processor, there are two design approaches that may be adopted, single-bit buffers and line scanning.

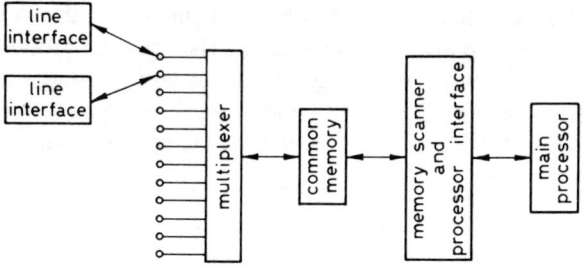

Fig. 4.20

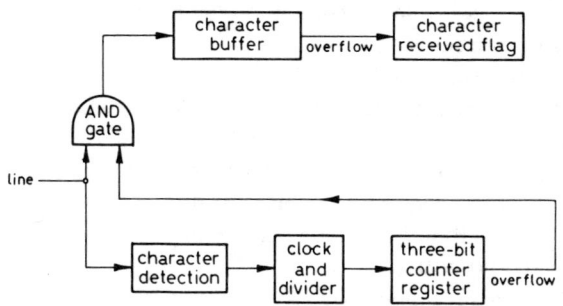

Fig. 4.21 Line interface in common memory system

(a) Single-bit buffers. This is the same as in the common memory approach above, except that the memory of the communication processor is used. The processor is used to assemble each character and for communication control with the large processor. The bits received from the lines can be transferred to the communication processor's memory, either through a direct-to-memory access channel or under program control.

(b) Line scanning. The line-scanning approach is one that uses the communication processor to establish and maintain line synchronization, character assembly, and completed character detection. A significant saving is thus realized, since no line sychronization and character detection hardware are required. This technique demands the use of a communication-oriented machine with an execution time fast enough to enable a large number of lines to be handled. The incremental cost of adding a line to the system is very low compared with that for other techniques.

Synchronous line interfaces the logic design of interfaces to synchronous data sets is considerably easier than the design of an asynchronous interface, since there is no need for bit synchronization and sampling hardware. Synchronous data sets supply all the timing necessary to receive each bit as it is made available.

The difficulty is to design in the capability of communicating in the message formats used in synchronous communications. The communications industry has assigned control characters for message control, message heading, error detection, and correction. The most important of these control characters are listed below with a brief explanation as to their use and purpose.

SYN Used to provide message framing and synchronization.
SOH Start of header. Used to mark the beginning of a sequence of characters which typically would be routing information. The STX character terminates the heading.
STX Start of text. Used at the beginning of a sequence of characters which are to be treated as the data message.
ETX* End of text. Used to terminate text following STX.
ETB* End of transmission block. Used to divide the text into conveniently sized blocks for transmission.
EOT End of transmission.
ACK* Acknowledge. A character sent by the receiving station to the transmitting station to indicate successful reception of a message.
NAK* Negative acknowledge. Indicates unsuccessful receipt of a message.
ENQ* Enquiry. Used to request a predetermined response from a remote station. The information requested might be the address of the station, or the status of the output buffer.

Those characters marked with an asterisk are known as turn-around characters and are discussed below. In addition to control characters, parity checks are often placed at specific points in the transmission, typically just after ETX and ETB characters.

Before any message can be transmitted, synchronization must be established between transmitting and receiving stations. This is achieved by means of a synchronizing sequence generated by the transmitting station. This sequence will precede every data message. It could typically consist of three consecutive SYN characters. In any examples, we shall abbreviate this to a single SYN character.

Before the first data message, it is usual to solicit the status of the receiving station to ensure that it is ready to receive. Thus, the first transmission is

    SYN
    ENQ

The ENQ is a turn-around character, so that on receipt of ENQ the receiver becomes the transmitter. If the ENQ is not received, the transmitter sends out SYN ENQ regularly (say at half-second intervals) for a time and then, if no reply is forthcoming, 'times out'. That is, it shuts down and gives a visible and an audible warning to the operator. If the ENQ is received correctly, the receiver transmits

    SYN
    status character
    ACK

and reverts to the role of receiver on the turn-around character ACK. The transmitter, on receiving the ACK, turns-around and transmits the first message.

Messages may take one of the following forms. If less than the terminal buffer size:

    STX   text   ETX   parity character
    SOH   heading   STX   text   ETX   parity character

If longer than the buffer size:

    STX   text   ETB   parity character
    SOH   heading   STX   text   ETB   parity character

A copy of the transmitted data will be retained in the terminal buffer until an ACK character is received from the receiver. Turn-around occurs on ETX or ETB to await the ACK. The receiving station will perform a parity check on each character and check the parity character itself. The receiving station turns-around on the ETX or ETB and sends either

    SYN
    status character
    ACK or NAK

depending upon the success of the transmission.

The transmitting terminal will delete the buffer on receipt of ACK and then send the next message. If a NAK is received, the message currently in the buffer is retransmitted. If there is no response after a fixed time, the transmitter generates SYN, followed by ENQ at regular intervals. Should the ETX or ETB characters fail to be recognized by the receiver then neither ACK nor NAK will be generated and the receiver will await for the ENQ from the transmitter after a fixed time when the receiver will send NAK and this will cause retransmission.

When the total message has been sent, the transmitter sends

    SYN
    EOT

which closes the link. An example showing error recovery is given in Fig. 4.22.

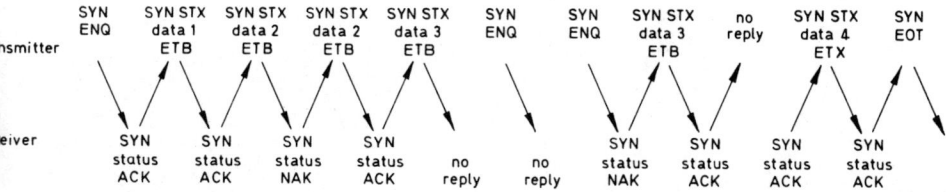

Fig. 4.22

If the main processor has to do all character decoding for each message, filter out the control characters, and check them, a significant percentage of processor time is spent doing communication formatting. However, if the processor has an instruction set that can efficiently perform this function, it is reasonable to handle a few lines in this way to avoid the cost of a hardware interface. The alternative approach of providing a hardware interface is expensive for a few lines but may pay off for many lines. However, it can result in limiting the application for which the interface can be used since it is then format-sensitive. An obvious solution is to use a communication processor for the job of handling the lines. Thus, the communication processor checks control characters and messages and sends out the appropriate acknowledgement. It may also communicate with the main processor on a message block basis and even have direct access to files.

5 System Management

5.1 Resource Allocation and Control

Within a time-sharing environment, the allocation and the control of the available resources is vital if effective utilization of the system is to be achieved. One of the major characteristics of the operation of a time-sharing system is the complete lack of control we have over which jobs will be run when. There is a total variability of job input and, unlike with a tradition batch-processing system, it is very difficult, in fact generally undesirable within the concept of time-sharing, to schedule specific types of jobs to certain periods during the day. Thus, with the near total flexibility offered to the time-sharing user, it is absolutely crucial that methods of control other than prescheduling are exercised to ensure that the system is able to maintain an acceptable service level to all users. Obviously, within such a volatile environment as time-sharing it is important that a large part of this control be automatic and generated by the system itself, once the control parameters have been determined and given to the system. Also, it is of course important that we have the ability to vary our control parameters easily as experience is gained with use of a given system.

One area of control which will be critical to any time-sharing installation is that of the allocation of file space to users. Naturally, an impossible situation would soon occur if users were allowed to build up indefinitely a variety of permanent on-line files on the available fast-access device(s). Human nature being what it is, it would take relatively little time before all the fast-access on-line file space was exhausted and the system ground to a halt. An analysis of this situation would soon reveal that in fact the majority of users were maintaining large areas of file space for storing information that was long since redundant. The initial solution to this problem is therefore to restrict the amount of on-line file space available to any user. Thus, if a user attempts to exceed the allocated file space, he is informed by the system and is therefore forced to analyse the information currently in his file store and delete any unwanted information in order to release file space for the new job. This is only a partial solution, since although it solves the critical problem of allocating on-line file space it does not solve the problem for the user who, when he has exhausted his on-line file space, does not have any redundant information in his files. A solution to this problem is to offer alternative file space on a less critical medium. On some configurations, this alternative storage could well be a cheap, relatively slow medium such as magnetic tape, or alternatively it could be on a much larger, relatively cheap, slow-access storage device such as a magnetic card file. However, in either case the principle is the same, to remove the strain on the file space available on the fast-access backing store and to offer alternative storage, albeit less readily accessable. Even so, the allocation and control of the fast-access on-line storage must be sufficiently flexible to allow the user who genuinely needs extra space the ability to obtain this space, provided it is available. A secondary method by which the allocation of file space can be controlled is by using some form of internal or, in the case of a time-sharing bureau, external charging scheme for the file space occupied. This will be a scaled charge to induce users to store permanent information on the least critical medium as far as the particular time-sharing system is concerned. For example, the highest unit charge would be made to users who exceeded the restricted level of file space on the fast-access on-line storage reducing to the lowest unit charge for off-line storage such as a magnetic tape. Naturally, built into the operating system will be the capability of logging the file space (on a suitable storage device) utilized by any user. These details can then be subsequently analysed by suitable accounting and budgeting programs.

The next area of control which is important in determining the performance of a time-sharing system is that of program size. Obviously, if a number of large programs were allowed to run during peak time-sharing loads, this would have a noticeably adverse effect on the performance of the system. In particular, with a high-performance multiprogramming and swapping system, the introduction of large programs into the system could mean the swapping of a number of other programs from memory in order to make room for these large programs. Also, while large programs are active in the system there would be a considerable increase in the swapping overheads. Therefore, there would be considerable degradation in the performance of the system, which would be reflected by the increase in the response times to all users. The effect of program size is perhaps not quite so critical if the system achieves time-sharing by a relatively simple and less responsive method such as 'fixed partition'. In this case, the partition itself places an absolute restriction on the memory space available, although, of course, a deterioration in system performance will again occur as a direct result of the increase in the swapping overhead.

A common solution is, as with file space, to restrict the maximum program size allowable. The operating system checks the main memory requirements of a program and rejects it if it is exceeding the maximum allowable size at a particular time. This solution is certainly not ideal and an alternative approach is for the scheduler to allocate the relevant program a low priority. This ensures that it runs infrequently and has only a limited effect on the time-sharing performance of the system. Naturally, the response time to the user running a large program will increase. Some systems output a message to the terminal user indicating that since the job is large the response time is likely to be longer than usual.

As with the allocation of file space, it is also useful (necessary in the case of a bureau) to employ a graduated charging system for memory space occupancy. The larger the program, the larger the unit charge. Again, the operating system will need the capability of logging main memory occupancy for each user job.

As we have seen in chapters 3 and 4, jobs with a long run time can also degrade the time-sharing performance of a system. These jobs may need to be swapped in and out many times and will often run for a full time-slice; both factors have a dertrimental effect on the performance and, in particular, the overall response time. Thus, run time is another area over which control must be exercised as part of the system management problem. The control of run time in fact depends very much on the scheduling process within the system and is considered more appropriately in the next section. Suffice to say that the effects of run time are handled most effectively if the system has the ability to vary, and in particular lengthen, the time-slice for long-running jobs and also to run these jobs less frequently, thereby reducing the overheads placed on the system by long running jobs. Although this particular area of control is essentially dependent on the scheduling algorithm, we must not overlook the need for effective control. Charging is again an important factor, as can be witnessed by the fact that the heaviest charges made by a time-sharing bureau are for central processor time, as this represents the user's utilization of the computer's real power.

A further area of control which can be important to a time-sharing installation is that of connection time. This is the time which a user is logged onto the system, regardless of whether he is performing useful work or not. In the case of a time-sharing bureau, each user connected to the system is charged for connection time. Users may not be charged in the case of an internal time-sharing service. Since the normal ratio of users to available lines for a time-sharing system is 3 : 1, it is important that some form of control is exercised over connection time. In the case of a bureau, they do not want customers to find they cannot get onto the system because all the access ports are in use. In the internal case, we do not want a situation to arise where a number of terminals are logged on to the system but are virtually unused, thus possibly preventing another more urgent user getting on to the system. A simple but effective method of control in the internal situation could be exercised by maintaining an analysis of total logged-on time for a particular user or terminal, against useful processing time. If this were then included in the normal budgeting and internal charging process, it would soon become obvious exactly which users (or even departments) were making excessive terminal demands yet producing little effective work!

Finally, as has already been indicated, one of the most important facets of system management is that of accounting and budgeting. It is obviously essential to produce periodic accounting data both for a monitoring function and as a charging basis. Thus we must be certain that when evaluating a time-sharing system the logging procedures are fully implemented, so that all the relevent accounting and budgeting information can be easily extracted. Naturally, in many cases, the programs that analyse the accounting data will have to be written by the installation.

In conclusion, when evaluating a time-sharing system, we must be convinced that the system control that can be placed on users, in terms of the allocation of resources, the control of those resources, and the subsidiary accounting facilities, are fully implemented to meet our particular needs.

5.2 Scheduling

The problem of job scheduling is one of the most important and fundamental design considerations in a time-sharing system. We must not underestimate the effect which the scheduling process will have on the efficiency of the computer system and on the efficiency of the user.

The design of a suitable scheduling algorithm can be an extremely complex task involving a thorough knowledge of the requirements of a time-sharing operation, as well as the use of statistical and queueing theory techniques. Certainly the fact that, in the main, the sequence, characteristics, and requirements of jobs to be processed are unknown in advance, makes it extremely difficult to design a scheduling algorithm that will satisfy all the users all of the time. There are, in fact, conflicting objectives in the design of a scheduling algorithm. The prime objective is to reduce as far as possible the average response time to all user demands. A further objective may be to ensure that the algorithm can differentiate between various levels of user job importance and urgency of service and establish a fair order of priority. It should therefore be obvious that, with even these few variables, there are numerous ways in which scheduling algorithms can be designed, since the design is dependent on the emphasis placed on a particular requirement, which in itself will be dependent on the user environment as well as on the method by which time-sharing is implemented. However, we shall now consider some possible scheduling algorithms and their consequences.

One of the simplest (and therefore the easiest to implement) algorithms is based on a circular queue of jobs and is commonly called 'round-robin' scheduling. In its most basic form, the time-slice is fixed and when a job has exhausted the time-slice or is held up awaiting input/output, the next job in the queue is activated and run. The process continues for all jobs in the queue in turn, until eventually we arrive at the starting point in the queue and the whole cycle is repeated. Unfortunately, this is only part of the story, as even with this basic 'round-robin' process the scheduler must distinguish between two classes of jobs: those jobs which have exhausted the time-slice and are therefore in an immediately 'runnable' state, and those which are awaiting input/output and are in a 'non-runnable' state. This distinction is vital, since in the latter case an input/output buffer must be maintained during the activation of other jobs.

If the system operates one 'round-robin' queue then we certainly have a simple scheduling process, but one which takes no account of job priorities or job characteristics. For example, relatively short computational jobs and those which have a noticeable amount of input or output are being penalized at the expense of the longer computational jobs, since each job has the same waiting time within the job queue. Similarly, we have no ability within the system to allocate priorities to urgent jobs, undoubtedly a serious drawback. Thus, the first conclusion we can draw is that even a simple approach to scheduling must include as a first priority a means by which the system, via the scheduler, can itself determine which job is to be run next. This approach is fundamental if we are to improve the overall serviceability of the system.

An initial improvement which we can make in the scheduling process, yet still maintain the basic principle of a round-robin technique, is to introduce more than one level of priority; the aim in the first instance is to distinguish between jobs requiring small amounts of computation with fast response and those requiring relatively large amounts of computation. In practice, it is necessary to maintain a number of round-robin queues (or levels). A job which utilizes a full time-slice is transferred to the next lowest level (i.e. queue), unless of course it is already at the lowest level. Hence, the long computational jobs will not be serviced as frequently as the shorter jobs or those calling for input or output during their time-slice. With this approach, we are cutting down the overhead associated with continuously swapping long-running jobs and improving the response to the shorter jobs, naturally at the expense of the longer jobs. Since, in a time-sharing environment, the majority of jobs tend to be of short duration, this approach is certainly a valid one. However, the penalty placed on long-running jobs is excessive, as these jobs will receive a relatively small amount of the central processor time, and also as a result will remain active in the system for considerable periods of time. Therefore, to improve the algorithm and allocate these long jobs a fairer share of the available time, considerable advantages will accrue if we have the capability of varying the time-slice. Corbato proposed and implemented for the Compatible Time-Sharing System (CTSS) at MIT such a multilevel scheduling system. In this system, jobs allocated to a lower priority level are given a longer time-slice when next activated. Thus, large jobs are run less frequently but, to compensate for this, receive more central processor time. In this way, the large jobs are being swapped less frequently and are thus placing less demands on the swapping capacity of the system, yet at the same time are receiving longer time-slices, which ensures they do not remain active in the system for excessive periods of time. A further refinement was introduced into the CTSS algorithm, in that the level to which a large job was allocated also depended upon the main memory it occupied, the larger jobs being allocated to a lower level. As was pointed out earlier, a direct result of this type of scheduling algorithm is that it favours short jobs and jobs which reach an input/output wait within the standard time-slice. This fact is directly compatible with the requirements of the majority of time-sharing users, and is certainly a necessity in terms of system efficiency. As we discussed in chapter 3, there is a requirement for having as short an overall time-slice as possible in conjunction with keeping the swapping overhead as low as possible, in order to keep the average response time to user requests as short as possible.

So far, all the concepts outlined in designing a suitable scheduling algorithm are valid, whatever the method employed to achieve time-sharing. In the case of a simple method of implementing time-sharing, such as 'fixed partition', the choice to be made by the scheduling algorithm is relatively simple—which job should be loaded next. However, in a multiprogramming or paging environment the choice is not so simple, since we are now very much concerned with main memory allocation as part of the scheduling process. Thus, there is a considerable increase in complexity in designing an effective scheduling algorithm. It is now necessary to decide whether a new job is to be loaded and, if necessary, which job or jobs should be swapped out in order to make room for the incoming job. Alternatively, a new job need not be loaded and instead another job currently resident activated. Further complications arise as a result of the variability of program size, since we must also aim to optimize main memory utilization and this can result, as we have seen in chapters 3 and 4, in a different emphasis being placed on the choice of which job is to be run next.

In the first place, a scheduling algorithm can be designed to satisfy one of two philosophies: either to activate as far as possible a job currently in main memory and swap jobs in and out only when absolutely necessary (e.g. when a job in memory has terminated or there is a higher priority job awaiting processing which is non-resident); or alternatively to always try and swap out jobs which have received a full time-slice. (Note that one would generally try to hold in memory jobs awaiting input/output so that the supervisor burden of managing input/output was reduced.) In the first case, the system will give a fast response to jobs resident in main memory, but there will be some delay before non-resident jobs get an opportunity to run. In the second case the system is attempting to give all jobs a fair share of the available central processor time, at a cost of increased swapping overhead and hence some degradation in overall response times. Which approach is adopted would depend to some extent upon the swapping capability of the system and also upon the general user job characteristics of a given system under operational conditions. However, regardless of which of the above approaches is adopted, and in many cases a given system will offer both alternatives dependent on installation requirements, the scheduling algorithm has still to determine which job is to be run next and what swapping is to take place. As we have seen earlier, a multilevel priority structure in conjunction with a variable time-slice is likely to be utilized as the basis for determining which job is to be run next. However, as we saw in chapter 3, the scheduling algorithm must take into account the current state of the main memory utilization. For example, when a new job is to be swapped in it will be necessary to determine which job currently in memory is the best candidate for swapping out (assuming room has to be made for the incoming job). If the job currently waiting to be swapped in requires more space than can be gained by swapping out one job, it may well be preferable to look further down the current job queues in order to find a job of reasonable priority but of smaller size that will involve the minimum amount of swapping for it to be loaded. Obviously, if this is the case then the scheduler must be aware that a particular job has been passed over and hence allocate this job maximum priority to ensure that, regardless of the subsequent main memory situation, this job gets run in the immediate future. Naturally, at some stage the above situation will arise and then the scheduling algorithm is further complicated, as it must now determine—depending on the current main memory utilization—how this large job is to be fitted into main memory. This may then well involve relocation of jobs in main memory (in a standard multiprogramming system) and the assessment of the best jobs for swapping.

Most scheduling systems in a multiprogramming environment do in fact differentiate between types of jobs under three broad categories: highly interactive, semi-interactive, and background. Hence a priority structure is allocated accordingly. This priority structure results in the highly interactive jobs tending to receive proportionately more processor time than the others. This is vital if a good response to interactive jobs is to be maintained.

Further complications in the design of a scheduling algorithm can arise if the system utilizes re-entrant software. For example, in the case of re-entrant compilers, an algorithm may well take into account not only the job priorities discussed but also the compilers that specific jobs require. The scheduler will then endeavour to load into main memory jobs requiring the same compiler, so that space is not wasted holding a number of different compilers. In this way, more jobs can be resident and the overall response time considerably improved. Naturally, this process of job grouping would still have very much to depend on the relative job priorities (i.e., it would generally not be practical to load a low priority in advance of a higher-priority job, just because it requires a currently resident compiler).

So far, we have made no direct reference to the scheduling of background batch-processing jobs. In the case of a system utilizing a fixed background partition, a straightforward priority queue with jobs run to completion is all that is normally required. Although, of course, it is necessary to have associated with the priority system a means of allocating urgent jobs specific 'deadlines'. In this way, one can ensure that these jobs are run before a given time. In a multiprogramming environment, these background jobs compete directly with the interactive jobs. It is therefore normal to allocate background jobs a low priority but increase their time-slice. This process, of course, should be readily modifiable by, if necessary, increasing the priority of specific background jobs of some urgency (over and above their normal queue priority). One obvious conclusion can be drawn from the above. In a multiprogramming system, if the aim is to give fast response to a large number of interactive users (i.e., the goal of timesharing) then we must expect some degradation in batch-processing throughput, the amount of degradation being ultimately dependent upon the philosophy inherent in the scheduling algorithm.

Let us now briefly consider the problems of devising scheduling algorithms within a paging environment. In the case of a memory mapping system, then, the problems associated with scheduling are in general, very similar to those outlined for a traditional multiprogramming system. However, with paging, the complexity of the scheduling algorithm will again increase, since we are now concerned with not only the scheduling of complete programs, but also the relevant active pages. As we have seen in chapter 3, not only does job priority play a significant part in the scheduling algorithm, but also the choice of which page should be swapped out also becomes critical (even more so than normal job swapping in a multiprogramming system) if the system is to maintain maximum efficiency and keep the swapping overhead as low as possible. Currently, the majority of algorithms are very much experiemental, but tend to operate on the basis of swapping either the longest resident page, or the least-accessed but longest-resident page. This process operates in conjunction with a normal multilevel job priority structure. Experiments are being carried out with more complex algorithms for page swapping based on the recent pattern of activity within the system. There is no limit to the complexity that can be introduced into the design of a scheduling algorithm, but increased complexity brings with it increased system overheads. When evaluating the suitability of a particular computer system, we should seriously question just how sophisticated the scheduling need be for a particular environment. We are sure many readers will feel they are capable of suggesting many further possibilities which could be included in a scheduling algorithm (i.e., such as a measure of time elapsed since a job was last processed—which is, of course, included in many algorithms). This fact alone is indicative of the number of possible algorithms that could be derived, and hence emphasizes the difficulty of establishing an algorithm which is not too complex but which will satisfy the majority of situations.

Finally, it is important that we realize that the design of a scheduling algorithm will influence to a great extent the way in which the system is used. For example, if the algorithm favours a pariticular class of job, and as we have seen this is commonly the case, then one is making the system attractive for specific types of work and therefore, indirectly, specific types of users. We are thus (via the scheduling algorithm) in a position to determine the type of use that will be made of a given system. We must certainly not overlook this fact in evaluating the merits of otherwise of different systems to satisfy the requirements of a particular environment and its associated community of users.

5.3 System Protection

Protection against some system failure is of prime importance in any computer installation. In particular, it is absolutely vital that there is some secondary means by which files can be re-created in the event of their loss, due perhaps, for example, to a disc failure which prevents their being retrieved. As we discussed in the previous section, most time-sharing systems will maintain a hierarchy of file storage and therefore it is natural that any method of system recovery is likely to be closely interfaced with the general problem of file storage. It is perhaps worth noting at this point that, in some ways, the problem of system protection in a time-sharing environment is more critical than in a traditional batch-processing system. This results mainly from the fact that operating an interactive environment means that original input is not readily, if at all, available. For example, in a batch-processing system, input will often be derived from some permanent medium such as punched cards, and therefore, as a last resort, it is possible to utilize this input (provided, of course, it has been retained for a reasonable period of time) to reinstate or update damaged or lost files.

There are two distinct problems to be considered with regard to system protection. The first is that of ensuring there is an adequate method of archiving or dumping information regularly, so that in the event of system failure the reinstatement of as much information as possible is feasible. Secondly, there must be a viable recovery procedure following a system failure which will ensure that the regeneration of file information is carried out as accurately and as automatically as possible.

The simplest method of maintaining a limited form of file security is to copy (i.e. dump) the entire file store at predetermined intervals of time onto a secondary storage medium, such as magnetic tape, Thus, if a system failure does occur all the file information on the current dump tape(s) can be reinstated. However, the dumping of the complete file will be a time-consuming operation and is therefore unlikely to be carried out more frequently than daily or, with a large file store, more likely weekly. Thus, when a system failure does occur, users could lose at worst a complete day's or week's work. Also, with this method all files are being copied, since a large number will not have changed between dumps an unnecessary amount of copying is being undertaken. A much better solution to the problem of file protection is known as *incremental dumping*. There are many sophisticated techniques which can be employed with incremental dumping, depending on the file structure and, to a certain extent, the system configuration. However, the basic principle is the same, that is to dump on to a secondary storage medium at short intervals (say every 15 to 30 minutes) all new and modified files. In this way, all relevent file information is preserved, unnecessary copying of inactive files is avoided, and at worst only a limited amount of work can be lost (a maximum of half an hour if a dump is taken at half-hourly intervals). The disadvantage of incremental dumping is of course the fact that it is being carried out regularly at short intervals, and therefore placing an extra load on the system while dumping takes place. This, we would suggest, is a small price to pay for the greatly improved file security of the system.

Whichever file-dumping method is employed (and many installations will naturally modify their file-dumping procedure to meet their individual file security requirements), the dump file will collect over a period of time a large amount of redundant information in the form of versions of files of which there is a more recent copy. It is therefore necessary to undertake a periodic reorganization of the dump file in order to purge the file of the unwanted information, and also to prevent it attaining unmanageable proportions.

An important facet of file protection is the maintenance of the individual user file directories, since these will contain pointers to all the copies of each user's files, regardless of where they are currently stored in the file store. Therefore the file directories represent what is probably the most valuable information in the system, and as such should certainly be stored in more than one part of the system, thus giving added safety in the event of a system failure. Similarly, the location of file directories on the dump file should also be recorded and be readily available. A periodic listing, showing where all files and file directories are to be found on the dump file can also be invaluable in critical system failure situations.

Recovery from a system failure and the design of the procedures to implement recovery is never trivial, and therefore should be designed into the system from the outset. Obviously, no recovery procedure can ever be foolproof, but it should certainly be designed to recover from all forseeable error conditions.

Let us consider some factors that we should try to allow for when designing recovery procedures.

Firstly, when a failure occurs we must accept (and therefore plan accordingly) that it is likely that those jobs which were active at the time of failure will be corrupted or lost. Also, it is important that active buffer areas are made consistent in terms of structure, although not necessarily accurate, so that the recovery can follow an ordered pattern. For example, any inconsistency in file directory information could mean that some areas on disc, say, would become effectively lost to the system following a failure. In this case, a solution would be to allocate these areas as free space even though a user file may well be lost as a result. If there is a significant failure and it is necessary to reinstate, say, the on-line disc file(s), it will be necessary to reload the file directories and all the associated files. Since activity will have occurred between dumps, we must realize that files which were created between dumps will almost certainly be lost, as these will in most cases be occupying areas on the disc that had been freed and hence reused since the last dump. Thus, when we reload from the dump file, the original file structure, at the last dump, will be reconstituted and the new file areas will be overwritten. Therefore, an important part of the recovery procedure will be to inform terminal users of the status of the system and the type of recovery undertaken, so that where possible individual users will be able to undertake recovery action themselves, such as calling for an older version of a lost file, which could well still be available since dump file reorganization would be infrequent. Bear in mind that, in the case of a minor failure, when there is little effect on the on-line storage situation, a full recovery from the dump file is unlikely to be necessary and only those jobs active at the time of failure will be lost. It is therefore important that the recovery procedures can automatically undertake the necessary checks in order to determine whether a full recovery cycle is needed. Naturally, in the case of a major failure, operator intervention may be necessary in order perhaps to load the requisite dump file onto the system. It is also important to note that software associated with file recovery should be extremely tolerant of poorly structured records. That is, it should be able to accept, for example, incomplete records which may not have standard terminators and which may yet still be capable of at least partly reconstructing the file, as any assistance given to the user in this way is better than no assistance at all.

Finally, the need for effective system protection cannot be over-emphasized, for without it the system would almost certainly be unworkable. Thus, although good file security may well place quite severe demands on the system and will reduce the overall performance and capability of the system to some extent, this fact must be accepted if a viable system is to be implemented.

5.4 Installation

The major problems of installing a computer system are standard, regardless of the type of system being implemented. We can broadly categorize these installation problems into three main areas. First there are the problems associated with pre-installation site preparation which involves such things as establishing a suitable computer site, air-conditioning requirements, false flooring, electrical supplies, fire protection, soundproofing, and, naturally, general office planning Second come the arrival and physical installation of the equipment, followed by the detailed acceptance necessary before the equipment is legally handed over to the new owner. Finally, system test-out procedures must be undertaken by the user installation before the equipment is given over to operational running.

All these various facets of installation which concern the establishment of the new equipment must obviously be prepared well in advance of machine delivery, and must certainly not be dismissed lightly as a minor irritation prior to the anticipated joys of operational running. Those readers who require practical guidance on the standard problems of installation and suggested solutions we would refer to the various computer manufacturers' installation manuals, or alternatively to the numerous books available on computer management and data processing. For our part, let us consider some of the installation problems peculiar to a time-sharing system (or, of course, in many cases, to any on-line interactive system).

One of the first problems associated with the installation of a time-sharing system stems from the fact that the majority of users are communicating directly with the system, either over local lines or by utilizing the common carrier facilities. Assuming that the initial number of lines and the associated line speeds have been chosen accurately to satisfy the needs of the particular installation, the fact that we intend to install a system dependent upon the communications subsystem means that we must ensure that all the aspects associated with communications are thoroughly tested prior to operational running. For example, it is important that all the communications handling routines are tested under near-operational conditions to ensure they perform in the manner expected, are as durable as anticipated, and in particular, handle error states effectively. Although most of these functions will have been tested prior to the delivery of the machine, probably on one of the manufacturer's own computers. It is true to say (and this applies to virtually all aspects of testing) that the experiences one gains using another computer, which will probably be a totally different configuration to that being delivered, never completely reflects the performance of the particular system when installed. Also, many installations may well have found it necessary to write at least parts of the communications software in order to satisfy particular requirements. In this case, the need for accurate pre-operational testing is even more vital.

Many time-sharing systems, as mentioned earlier, utilize a communications processor as a 'front-end' machine for handling a large part of the communications function. If this is the case, it may well be worth considering having this part of the system delivered some time in advance of the main system. In this way, one can gain invaluable experience and undertake considerable testing of the communications aspect of the operation, without having the problems associated with the main system to deal with at the same time. This approach would also be particularly valuable if some of the communications software has been user-written.

An extension to the technique of initially undertaking local testing on devices which will be eventually remote from the main centre is particularly significant if we are installing a remote job entry system. For example, if the system is to support a number of fast remote devices, such as card readers and line printers, it would be sensible to initially check-out the functioning of these devices in-house prior to installing them at their eventual remote locations. In this way, thorough testing of all aspects of the use of the remote job entry terminal, under ideal local conditions can be carried out. Any errors arising in either terminal communication or message handling can readily be seen and the necessary corrective measures undertaken. Naturally, in practice, only one of the remote job entry terminals would be tested locally, since we can assume, with some degree of confidence, that if the major parts of the system are functioning correctly for one terminal then all others should operate in a similar manner.

With a time-sharing system we are relying not only on the serviceability of a few major compilers plus local hardware, as can be the case with some batch-processing systems, nor only on the traditional software, but also on a large amount of specialist software such as editors, dynamic debugging facilities, specific on-line languages, and sophisticated operating systems. Also, there are the associated problems of scheduling, swapping, time-slicing and dynamic file handling. It is therefore crucial that the procedures for basic system test-out are as detailed as is humanly possible. We must check every aspect of possible system use to ensure that all the software and hardware functions in the manner expected. For example, one area which is often not checked as thoroughly as it might be is that of the dumping and recovery procedures. Yet the need to ensure that the procedures work effectively and to gain an understanding in practice of how these procedures operate is vital, if total confusion is to be prevented when the need to use these facilities arises operationally.

As has been outlined, a time-sharing system is particularly vulnerable to the performance of the operating system. In particular, the success of the operation depends upon the accuracy of the file-handling routines within the operating system. It is therefore extemely important that efficient routines are devised (well before the system is delivered) to test all the facets of the operating system upon which efficient running of the system depends. These routines should check the majority of user facilities and attempt, within the limits of feasibility, to 'break' the operating system. In this way, we should be able to pinpoint possible areas of weakness and therefore be in a position to ensure that the less tolerant parts of the system are if possible rewritten. Alternatively, probably as a stop-gap, ensure that users are informed of facilities which as a result of testing may not be immediately available, thus preventing users from obtaining access to the parts of the operating system which may cause undesirable 'crashes' in the early days of operational running (one may also consider, as further security, 'locking out' by program those parts of the system to which user access is to be prevented). A fundamental philosophy which is relevant to the installation of a computer system is that it is far better to give users restricted facilities that operate effectively than the full facilities which could give rise to unexplained errors. The installation management is selling the system to the users, and lack of confidence from the outset, due to unexplained errors, has a much more permanently damaging effect than that created by causing a little initial inconvenience by placing restrictions on certain facilities.

Finally, users of a time-sharing system will in many cases be inexperienced computer users. They will often have little or no knowledge of how the system operates or of what facilities are available to them. Therefore, fundamental to the success of a given system will be how readily information is obtainable regarding both the use and the facilities of the system. To this end at least, user handbooks should be produced explaining clearly all the facets of the system, ranging from the basic principles of how to use the system to details of individual items of software. Many systems offer special programs, which a user can interrogate, which explain at the terminal various facilities of particular interest. For example, programs explaining how to use the system (for the first-time user) and specialist programs of the 'teach-yourself' variety will prove invaluable as a 'back-up' or substitute to normal user training and handbooks. We would suggest that effort expounded by the installation in producing further software of this nature (over and above that perhaps supplied by the manufacturer) will repay itself many times over during the life of the installation, if for no other reason than creating satisfied users, some of whom may be independent of support from staff at the central installation.

6 Evaluation

> Choose your love, and then love your choice.
> Proverb

6.1 Benchmarking

The process of benchmarking can be summarized as the need to derive suitable yardsticks by which valid comparisons between various systems can be made. A number of benchmarking techniques are applicable to any system, and in the main represent traditional approaches to system evaluation. For example, a Gibson mix or Post Office Work Unit (both a mix of computer instructions) can be utilized to establish a measure of the power of a particular computer. (The latter involves a mix of operations containing a few instructions and a calculation involving a measure of P.O.W.U.s performed per second per 1000 characters transfered. It is probably only suited to the evaluation of Post Office systems.) However, there is nothing magical about a Gibson mix or P.O.W.U. It may well be that a prospective user can devise a suitable mix of computer instructions that are more truly representative of the type of work a given system will undertake in practice. Should a prospective user feel that working to this level of detail is unnecessary (which is often the case), a fairly accurate approximation can be obtained from a comparison of word size and cycle time, possibly used in conjunction with quoted instruction times for selected instructions. In fact, the latter approach was the one we adopted and found satisfactory.

The traditional batch-processing technique, of obtaining the total elapsed time for a given job mix on a number of systems, can also be applied to obtain a first approximation of a system's job throughput capacity. Naturally, this approach is limited in application when considering fairly sophisticated systems, and the results must be viewed very conservatively. This is a direct result of the fact that the choice of job mix, the scheduling priorities of the operating system and the methods of implementation can distort the results considerably. However, if these points are carefully weighed, an initial estimate of a given system's overall capability can be derived.

In the remainder of this section, we shall consider in rather more detail particular aspects of benchmarking and evaluation.

Software evaluation. Here we are concerned with the programming languages available, the general-purpose systems programs such as editors, file manipulation packages, and debugging tools, software packages appropriate to one's needs, and the overall facilities provided by the operating system.

(a) One must obviously compare the range of programming languages offered by systems but, equally importantly, one must compare the quality of the compilers. The size of a compiler and the size of object code produced by it is important for a number of reasons. The smaller a program (compiler or object program), the less is the demand upon the swapping channel. In a multiprogramming environment, the smaller a program, the more memory space there is for the other jobs in the mix. The size of compilers will be quoted by the manufacturer. In order to measure the size of object programs, it is necessary to construct a set of programs representative of the type of programs that will be run on the system. This set of programs should be compiled and the resultant object code measured.

One may also like to measure the run-time efficiency of the object code. Once again, the set of typical programs should be used. The time to compile and run the set should be measured. One must be very careful to ensure that the times recorded represent the same series of events on all systems. Perhaps the easiest method is to run each job on its own (i.e., uniprogrammed) and measure the elapsed time of each job.

Finally, one should consider the level of the language which has been implemented. In the case of FORTRAN, say, there are well-defined levels of the language to which manufacturers adhere. In the case of BASIC and JOSS, this is not currently the case, and a comparison should be made of the various implementations.

In all attempts to evaluate compilers, one should remember that the tests devised are never truly representative of the actual situation that will prevail. Before making any measurements, one should be clear that the results will give valid and useful information. It is not very comforting to obtain a system with the most efficient language X compiler, only to find that, because the facilities offered by language Y are so much better for a time-sharing environment, language X is seldom used by your users.

(b) General-purpose system software is rather more difficult to evaluate, but one should certainly pay attention to the editing and debugging facilities provided and evaluate their power and ease of use.

(c) Software packages are obviously very application-oriented, but should be evaluated very much like compilers, under the headings of efficiency and facilities.

(d) The evaluation of the operating system as a whole should be considered under a number of headings—ease of use (i.e., the user interface), range of facilities (e.g., concurrent batch, the ability to support special-purpose terminals such as graphics and remote batch terminals), and flexibility (e.g., ability to add new commands, to allow users to define their own commands). The success of a time-sharing system is very much a function of the operating system and one must contrast the facilities offered with the efficiency of operation. Thus, a simple system will often support more simultaneous users than a sophisticated system, simply because the price of sophistication is an increased overhead.

Hardware evaluation. Here we are concerned with two aspects of the hardware—speed and expandability. In a sense, the speed of the central processor is unimportant on its own, since the run-time of a given program is as much a function of the software quality as of the hardware speed and will be measured (if such a measurement is carried out) when testing the compilers. The speed of the peripherals will also be taken into account when measuring such things as compilation speeds, since most systems will make extensive use of disc when compiling. Similarly, if input and output are included in any program timing then the card reader and line printer speeds will have been included.

There are obvious peripheral speeds which are critical, such as the swapping device latency and transfer rate, since this is central to the whole concept of time-sharing, or the line printer rate for high volume output. Some systems will have other critical speeds relevant to the particular application, but these should be obvious and easy to measure.

The expansion of the system is an important factor. Thus, one should see how main memory may be expanded, how the on-line filing system may be increased, and how the central processor power may be increased by either installing a faster processor or by adding more processors. One should ensure that not only are hardware expansions possible, but that the software will support the expansions. Thus, for example, if you plan to add a second drum on a second channel, ensure that the software is able to utilize it to its fullest advantage.

Time-sharing benchmarking. The main problem in benchmarking a time-sharing system is deciding what to measure and how to set about measuring it. Let us consider two factors which one could measure.

(a) Response time. Here, the measurement consists of timing the response at one or more terminals with a given load on the system, over a period of time. There are a number of parameters which one can vary. One may control the number of active terminals, the range of languages and utility programs in the job mix, and the type of activity being timed.

One should attempt to arrange to have as many terminals as one is envisaging on the proposed system available for the benchmark. This presents a number of problems. If the proposed number is large, one has to have a large number of people available to conduct the benchmark and it must be carefully planned and recorded. A further difficulty may arise in that the manufacturer may not be able to provide more than a few terminals for the purpose of the benchmark. Since extrapolation from few to many terminals is a risky exercise, one should try and settle for a common number, as high as possible, which all maufacturers can supply. In this way, one is measuring the same thing on all systems under consideration. If the difference between the proposed number of terminals and the number available for the test is large, the validity of the test is questionable. If a manufacturer is unable to supply sufficient terminals, this may be an indication of that manufacturer's attitude to time-sharing!

Having fixed the number of terminals, one must now decide what to run at each terminal. If one is attempting to measure the overall capability of the system, any general mix of jobs will suffice. If one is trying to simulate a particular load, then obviously more care must be taken in selecting the activity at each terminal. If the number of terminals is fewer than the number proposed, then one should ensure that the jobs running at each terminal are non-trivial to compensate for this. On some systems, it is possible to set a job running from a terminal and then detach the terminal from the job and use the terminal for another job. Obviously, the detached job must be such that it can run without intervention from the terminal. This facility may allow the benchmark to be run from a single terminal.

The final consideration is what is to be measured at one or more of the terminals. One might measure the response to trivial jobs, such as simple editing functions, to ensure that delays do not occur at this level. One might measure the response to an interactive job which, say, reads data from the terminal, does a trivial computation, outputs the results to the terminal, and then loops back for more input. In such a case, the time between supplying the data and receiving the results is of particular interest. When carrying out timings, one should repeat them a number of times to ensure that no large fluctuations occur.

Unless one carries out extensive tests to measure the response under varying conditions of a variety of jobs, one is unable to cover all likely response situations. However, if one is careful in choosing the conditions, the responses obtained under these conditions should be indicative of the general response level.

Over and above any regulated test conditions, a great deal of information may be obtained by using a terminal into a system under normal time-sharing conditions, either on a customer's premises or at the manufacturer's (if the manufacturer uses time-sharing in-house—always a good sign!).

(b) Concurrent batch processing. Here, the measurement is concerned with two things—the effect of concurrent batch processing upon the mean response time (or what amounts to the same thing, the effect on the number of terminals

which can be supported with concurrent batch with a given mean response time), and the batch throughput. One might use the same terminal environment as before and add one or more batch streams. The measurements would be the response time as before, and the elapsed time for the batch jobs to complete. The problem with such a benchmark, where two separate measurements are being taken, is to correlate the two sets of results. Thus, what inferences are to be drawn if system A has a mean response time of six seconds and an elapsed batch time of 12 minutes and system B has a mean response time of eight seconds and an elapsed batch time of nine minutes? Therefore, before conducting such a test, one must be sure that the results are going to be useful and that conclusions can be drawn from the results.

A benchmark. A benchmark we have used in the selection of a time-sharing system is described below. We were selecting an initial system capable of supporting (with a short response time) at least 30 terminals simultaneously. The maximum number of terminals available on some of the systems we were evaluating was 10, so we standardized on this number of terminals for our test. In order to compensate for the low number of terminals, we arranged that nine of the terminals should be running medium-sized (5–10K), compute-bound jobs. This ensured that jobs were constantly being swapped in and out. At the tenth terminal, we ran an interactive program and measured the response between supplying the data and receiving the results. This had the advantage that it was a simple situation to set up, since the same job could be run at each of the nine terminals. By choosing a job which was in an infinite loop for the nine terminals, we also ensured the environment was constant for the period of the measurements at the tenth terminal. Although this benchmark is very crude, it proved highly effective.

Wherever possible, we ran as many simultaneous jobs as possible to a maximum of 30 and measured the response of our interactive program as a check, and these correlated with the results for 10 very well.

Finally, one of the best and simplest ways of measuring response time is to sit down at a terminal of an operational system with about the right number of users logged in and put the system through its paces for an hour or two.

6.2 Case Study

In this section, we shall consider how we conducted in practice, an evaluation of available time-sharing systems to meet our particular requirements (an educational environment with a large population of users running numerous interactive but relatively trivial programs). Naturally, the emphasis placed on particular system aspects considered vital for the success of the installation would not be the same in another situation, where perhaps the demands placed on a system are of a different nature. However, the procedures and principles adopted for the evaluation would be valid in any situation. It is this area of technique which we wish to emphasize and which the reader may find relevant, should he be confronted with the problem of system evaluation.

Before discussing in detail the manner in which an evaluation can be conducted, one point in particular should be stressed. Unless the prospective user is inexorably tied to a given manufacturer, we would strongly recommend that at least limited initial discussions be carried out with as many suppliers of equipment as possible. This can be a relatively painless task if undertaken methodically, and will be of immense benefit to the prospective user in ensuring that the system which would best meet particular requirements is not eliminated without a hearing. This latter point is very relevant when one is evaluating a fast-developing area such as time-sharing. The process of establishing a 'short list' of manufacturers with whom detailed evaluation procedures would be undertaken can be carried out in the following way. A short summary of the particular needs, emphasizing the broad outline of minimum requirements that a proposed system would have to meet (including a realistic financial limit) should be circulated to all possible manufacturers. Associated with this document should be a deadline (of say one month), by which time any manufacturer who is in a position to meet the outline minimum requirements must have lodged an official 'request to tender'. We found that in this way (along with some initial discussion of course), those manufacturers who either could not meet the financial limit or could not satisfy the minimum requirements (bearing in mind that a detailed evaluation would follow) were eliminated fairly rapidly. Thus, as a result of this initial pruning, a 'short list' is derived and one can feel confident that no system has been overlooked.

The next phase of detailed evaluation will naturally be a considerably longer process than the derivation of an adequate 'short list'. This phase is likely to consist of at least four major elements: exhaustive discussions with the manufacturers and the testing of their claims (including, of course, the use of a standard benchmarking test, as has been outlined in the previous section), the establishment of a detailed and reasonable minimum specification, presentations by the manufacturers of their proposals prior to the final submission and, in conclusion, the assessment by the evaluation team of the tenders.

Let us consider the above elements in the order listed.

The meetings with the manufacturers and the process of assessing their claims can be a difficult task unless considerable determination is shown by the assessors. It is important if we are to obtain a valid evaluation that a number of basic hurdles are overcome as far as possible. Firstly, we must ensure we meet the right people within the manufacturing organization; in particular, it is essential to get behind the sales and systems 'front men' if a detailed technical evaluation is to be totally successful. For example, much can be learned by talking 'off the cuff' to, say, the systems programmers who are or were responsible for the implementation of major software modules. Secondly, when benchmarking a system, try to ensure tests are carried out on configurations which parallel, as far as is feasible, the type of configuration that is likely to be proposed.

Particularly dangerous inaccuracies can arise, if tests are carried out on a much more powerful machine within a manufacturer's range, and then attempts are made to extrapolate back in order to try and arrive at more realistic results. Also, the importance of visiting similar user installations (where possible) cannot be overemphasized, for it is in this environment that it is possible to discover such things as: the overall reliability of the system, the performance of specific software elements (e.g., operating system, compilers, etc.), and also the general technical competence and service level of the particular manufacturer in the 'live' rather than 'sales' situation. However, one should avoid being over influenced by the user installation which for one reason or another is obviously biased heavily for or against the supplier of their particular equipment (although to meet the latter will take considerable initiative on the part of the evaluation team). Documentation at this stage is, of course, vitally important and all events and findings should be clearly and carefully recorded.

The drawing up of a realistic minimum specification must be carefully undertaken, since in its final form it represents clear terms of reference for both the manufacturer and the evaluation team. Appendix 6.1, represents a sample specification designed to meet specific time-sharing requirements (these requirements would, of course, differ in another situation). Naturally, the specification represents, as far as the evaluation team are concerned, the ideal minimum. However, this does not mean that all (any) of the manufacturers will be able to satisfy every condition totally. The final selection of a particular system will have to take into account other vital factors outside the minimum specification, such as cost/performance, customer service, etc.

Inevitably, during the evaluation process there are likely to be presentations of proposals prior to the final submission of the reports and tenders. If these presentations are to be effective as far as the proposed user is concerned, careful control must be exercised over the format of the presentation. In this way, two major objectives will be satisfied. Firstly, each presentation will supply the information considered relevant to the prospective user. Secondly, each presentation will follow an ordered and similar format. These two points are particularly relevant, since in most cases the purpose of the presentations is to sell a given system, not only to the evaluation team (to whom large parts of the presentation will be irrelevant) but also to other significant decision-makers within the proposed user organization. It is therefore important that the evaluation team ensure that all the necessary information (in the requisite detail) is presented to the ultimate decision-makers (e.g., members of the board of directors, managers responsible for the ultimate control over the evaluation team, or governors and directors of an academic institution, etc.), so that they are in a position to assess fairly, and with some knowledge, the evaluation team's final conclusions. Thus, by combining the efforts of the evaluation team along with the controlling function of the overseeing committee (if it is in the form of a committee) an unbiased selection should hopefully result. Appendix 6.2 is an example of the type of document that can be circulated to manufacturers prior to the presentations.

It is to this document that all the presentations should, in the main, conform.

The final stage in the process of evaluation is the receipt of the manufacturer's written proposals and tenders and the subsequent drafting of the evaluation team's assessments and final conclusions. With the adoption of a minimum specification approach, much of the assessment can be conveniently documented in tabular form, utilizing cross-referencing to the minimum specification. Appendices 6.3, 6.4, and 6.5 indicate the type of information that can be extracted in a final report and assessment, using essentially a tabular format. The last section of the report would of course be a brief summary of conclusions, which highlights, by manufacturer, each system's major advantages and disadvantages, ultimately recommending a particular system.

With the above approach, we ensure that each system is carefully considered and that no major omissions occur. In a fast-developing field such as time-sharing, a carefully considered and documented evaluation is mandatory if the conclusions which are finally drawn are to be totally valid.

APPENDIX 6.1

Specification for a time-sharing computer system

Section A. General guidelines

A.1. Central computing system

The central computing system will have sufficient main memory and range of backing store to support the time-sharing/batch activity envisaged. The whole system will be capable of being economically updated to deal with a substantial increase in the number of terminals and expansion in the range of more sophisticated types of outstations. Time-sharing activity will have priority over batch activity in the allocation of the initial resources and probably in allocation of funds for expansion.

A.2. Software availability

The *current availability* of fully supported and *well-proven* time-sharing software (as indicated in section B) which has been *generally released* and *tested by a variety of users* for a significant period of time is regarded as being of the utmost importance.

A.3. Terminals

Initially, most terminals will be Teletype 33 (ASR). The distribution of these terminals is given in section A.4. It is intended that the central terminals will later be augmented by visual display units and then by CRT/light pen equipment and other special-purpose devices. It is also intended that the single terminals installed initially at various remote outstations will be augmented later by more terminals and then by remote batch terminals.

A.4. Terminal distribution

The computing system installed at phase 1 will be capable of supporting *at least* 30 terminals simultaneously on-line, during terminal activity as outlined in section B.5. The terminals will be distributed as follows:

    (a)   Thirity terminals will be connected locally.

    (b)   Eighteen terminals will be at remote sites and connected using the public switched-telephone network.

Where the system is unable to support all the terminals simultaneously, the terminals will be scheduled so that at least 30 terminals are connected to the system at any one time.

A.5. Initial system

It is *not* intended to install a system which is fully loaded and fully stretched in its performance at the day of installation, since this would allow nothing for the inevitable rapid expansion in computer demand which will occur. The system must initially have *some spare time-sharing* capacity.

Section B. Minimum requirements for the time-sharing computing system

It is essential that the following facilities be *generally released* for the proposed configuration six months before delivery unless otherwise stated below.

B.1. Languages at the terminals

(a)   FORTRAN IV or Algol 60.
(b)   Assembly language.
(c)   Text editing language. The text editing language must enable users to edit by reference to lines and/or by reference to characters.
(d)   Extended BASIC.
(e)   JOSS or an equivalent language.

Information must be able to be entered via the paper tape reader of a terminal as well as by direct keying.

B.2. Batch languages available at central computing system

(a)   Algol 60.
(b)   FORTRAN IV.
(c)   COBOL.
(d)   Assembly language.
(e)   a List-processing language.

Here *(a)* and *(e)* are preferably to be available now, but, if not, they must be generally released by at most six months after the installation of the computing system and a delivery date must be given with a statement of contractual obligation by the supplier.

B.3. Simultaneous activity

(a)　Simultaneous terminal activity and batch activity, using any combination of languages defined above in sections B.1 and B.2, respectively.
(b)　Initiation at a terminal of a background job in any language defined in section B.2 and subsequent interrogation to find the state of the initiated job.
(c)　The ability to detach a terminal from a job while it is running and use the terminal for another activity.
(d)　The ability to insert information on paper tape or cards at the central computing system during terminal activity and this information to be accessible from any one terminal.

B.4. Degree of interaction between any terminal user and the system with all terminal languages.

(a)　During the execution of at least an assembly code program, it must be possible temporarily to stop the program without disturbing it and then dump the values of selected variables, to set up a selective trace, to dump code and registers, to patch in object code, and to continue from any point in the program.
(b)　Each compiler must be able to return all the error messages directly to the terminal.
(c)　The object program must be able to take its data from the terminal at run time.
(d)　The object program must be able to output results direct to the terminal.

B.5. Response time at terminals with all languages listed in section B.1.

The computing system initially installed (both hardware and software) must cater for the following worst-case situation:
　　When 10 of the total number of at least 30 active terminals are simultaneously making non-trivial system demands (such as compilation or execution), one of the 10 programs is highly interactive. In this interactive program, the following actions occur *repeatedly*; data input from the terminal is followed by minimal computation and then output to the terminal. The average response time with this interactive program must not exceed three seconds. This response time is the elapsed time between the end of the terminal input and the start of the terminal output.

B.6. Filing system

(a)   Each user's files must be securely protected from other users by means of a user name and non-printing or masked password.
(b)   Each user must have the ability to share specified files among specified users and to specify modes of access on the files.
(c)   A library file or files for all languages listed in sections B.1 and B.2 must be accessible to all terminal and batch jobs.
(d)   Software to dump and restore files to protect the user in the event of hardware failure must be available.

B.7. Resource allocation and control

The system must allow on-line file space, program size, and run-time to be allocated and controlled.

APPENDIX 6.2

Agenda

1. Phase 1

1.1 Hardware
1.2 Terminal facilities available
1.3 Batch-processing facilities available
1.4 Other similar installations
1.5 Accomodation and installation
1.6 Hardware maintainance
1.7 Software support
1.8 Software completion dates before proposed installation date
1.9 Philosophy of implementation of terminal facilities.

2. Phase 2 and beyond

Guide to agenda items

1. Phase 1

In all cases, details should be given of *(a)* what is available now and *(b)*, clearly separate, what will be available before the proposed installation date.

1.1 *Hardware*

The items proposed should be given in the following order, with at least details of the characteristics indicated. In all cases cost and delivery dates should be given.

C.P.U.	model number, date at which first manufactured, number installed
main memory	size, speed, module size, maximum size
multiplexer	hardware/software capabilities, memory size, maximum line capacity
disc	transfer rate, latency, average access time, capacity, number proposed
disc control units	number proposed, any special features
magnetic tapes	transfer rate, 7- or 9-track, number proposed
magnetic tape control units	number proposed, any special features
other storage	details as for disc
slow peripherals	speeds and system demands

1.2 *Terminal facilities*

(a) Information will be entered via the paper tape reader of a teletype as well as by direct keying.

(b) The command language will normally be compatible with that of the batch-processing facilities of the system. It will be possible to use a terminal to communicate with programs running in backround mode.

(c) ALGOL or FORTRAN, BASIC, JOSS, and a low-level language should be available initially. Plans for the extension of the range of languages should be stated with completion dates.

(d) The provision of facilities for submitting, via a terminal, programs containing sections in more than one language is desirable.

(e) It is a firm requirement of the system that conversational facilities be available.

Conversational facilities include the following:

> The compiler sending all its error messages directly to the terminal.
> The object program able to take its data from the terminal at run time.
> An object program able to output its results direct to the terminal.

It is desirable that the object program may be stopped during execution, modifications made in source code, and the run continued from the break-point without a complete recompilation. Also, it is desirable that during the run of a program it should be possible to dump values of variables, run a selective trace, dump code, and registers, patch in object code, and other such debugging techniques. The method of implementation should be clearly stated (with indications on main memory use) under item 1.9 of the agenda.

(f) Information may be inserted on paper tape or cards at the central computing system and then all the usual activities take place at a terminal.

(g) The filing system should be such that each user's files are protected from other users. However, the system should be flexible enough to allow files to be accessed with the owners' permission.

(h) The system should provide accounting and use monitoring, to enable the resources to be allocated and controlled.

(i) A text-editing language should be available which enables users to edit either by reference to lines or by reference to characters.

Conversational languages available should be listed with compiler size and a definition of 'conversational'. Other languages available should be listed with compiler size and an indication of their use from a terminal.

1.3 *Batch-processing facilities*

It is expected that a full range of languages will be available for batch-processing use, including ALGOL, FORTRAN, COBOL, LISP, a simulation language, R.P.G., and a symbolic assembly language with full macro facilities. A comprehensive set of applications packages should be provided, e.g., information retrieval, critical path techniques, management games, stock forecasting, etc., with evidence of their development and current use. There should also be real evidence of plans to provide further applications facilities and other languages as they are more fully developed, e.g., PL/I, ALGOL 68, B.C.L. Proposed dates for completion of implementation should be given. Further, there should be special facilities associated with at least ALGOL and FORTRAN for rapidly processing a large number of very small program development runs submitted by students and staff (cf. WATFOR compiler). Batch processing languages available should be listed with compiler size.

1.4 *Other similar installations*

Details, as indicated below, should be given *only* of current installations of the system proposed in 1.1, with emphasis upon those satisfying the type of activity envisaged:

organization;
installation date;
configuration;
number of terminals used 'simultaneously';
total number of terminals;
details of terminal activity;
details of batch activity; and
details of bench mark runs.

1.5 *Accommodation and installation*

Brief details should be given of the following:

rooms sizes, including minimum heights;
air-conditioning requirements;
false floors;

false ceilings;
freight charges; and
installation costs.

1.6 *Hardware maintenance*

Details should be given of the following:

cost per annum (1 and 1½ shifts), including spares;
resident engineer and/or availability;
guaranteed period;
liability of supplier for down time and partial down time;
nearest service centre and number of maintenance engineers based there to deal with proposed system; and
system standby facilities available in the event of a major breakdown; in particular, support available during repair, to process the normal amount of batch activity plus batch for the normal time-sharing load.

1.7 *Software support*

The policy on software support, indicating the current effort available in various areas of development, should be clearly stated with a guaranteed period of continued maintenance. Areas of co-operation should be indicated. The availability of software documentation should be given, including explicit description of information available—e.g., listings, with or without commentary, flowcharts, system specifications, complete description of each segment.

1.8 *Software completion dates*

The completion dates of software due before the proposed installation should be given, together with an indication of the extent to which the supplier would be willing formally to admit a liability to supply.

1.9 *Philosophy of implementation of terminal facilities*

A brief description should be given of the general approach to the implementation of the conversational languages available at the terminals. The tasks carried out by the multiplexer (or equivalent) should be stated.

2. *Phase 2 and beyond*

Subsequent developments will include the addition of further teletypes and a small set of video display units. At a later stage, a CRT/light-pen will be added, together with remote batch terminals. A possible phased development scheme should be indicated with costings and the expected enhancement of performance at each stage.

APPENDIX 6.3

Ability of manufacturers to satisfy minimum specifications

Specification Paragraphs	Manufacturer				
	A	B	C	D	E
A.2	Y	*	Y	Y	*
A.4	Y	*	Y	*	Y
A.5	Y	*	*	Y	Y
B.1 *(a)*	Y	Y *	Y	Y	Y
(b)	Y	Y *	Y	Y	Y
(c)	Y	*	*	Y	Y
.					
.					
.					
.					

Note: * in this table refers to an associated table of comments (see below).
Y indicates that the specification item has been satisfied

Specification Paragraphs	Manufacturers	Comments
A.2	*B*	A non-robust version of BASIC was available in early 1968.
	E	Mark 1 operating system release date, etc.
A.4	*B & D*	Benchmark tests indicate that the system will not support, etc.
. . . .		

APPENDIX 6.4

Response Times at Terminals

Members of the department carried out benchmark tests, as defined in the Specification paragraph B.5.

Manufacturer	Configuration	Location/Date	System	No. of Users	Response Time in Seconds
A B C D E	Specification of basic configuration on which the benchmark tests were carried out.	Place(s) and Date(s) where tests were carried out.	Specification of the version of the operating system or special software module used for the test(s).	No. of users or jobs set running from available terminals during the test(s).	Response time recorded at the test terminal as defined in paragraph B.5 of the specification.

APPENDIX 6.5

Cost and Hardware Comparison

Note: throughout this document K is taken to mean 1024 and M is taken to mean K^2

	Manufacturer				
	A	B	C	D	E
Total purchase price					
Single shift maintenance					
Rental per month (5 year contract)					
Central processor					
Main memory in addressable units					
Main memory in K bits	This was used in order to obtain a relative measure of main memory size, thereby allowing for different word lengths.				
Cycle time in microseconds					
Time to access 288 bits in microseconds	Again used to relate cycle time to word length.				
Maximum main memory in K bits					
Maximum addressable main memory					

Bibliography

Adams, C.W. (1965). 'Responsive time-shared computing in business, its significance and implications', *AFIPS Conference Proc.*, **27**, 483.
Arbuckle, R.A. (1966). 'Computer analysis and thruput evaluation', *Computers Automn.*, Jan, 1966, 12.
Babcock, J.D. (1965). 'Man-machine interaction : conversational programming', *IFIP Congress 65 Proc.*, 544.
Baker, C.L. (1966). 'JOSS : introduction to a helpful assistant', Memorandum RM-5058-PR, RAND Corporation.
Barron, D.W., Fraser, A.G., Hartley, D.F., Landy, B., and Needham, R.M. (1967). 'File handling at Cambridge University', *AFIPS Conference Proc.*, **30**, 163.
Bryan, G.E. (1966). 'Introduction to the system implementation', RAND Corporation P-3486.
Bryan, G.E. (1967). 'User scheduling and resource allocation', RAND Corporation RM-5216-PR.
Clippinger, R.F. (1965). 'Experience in multiprogramming', *IFIP Congress 65 Proc.*, 362.
Coffman, E.G. (1968). 'An analysis of computer operations under running time priority disciplines', *Interactive Systems for Experimental Applied Mathematics*, 257, Academic Press.
Coffman, E.G., Varian, L.C. (1967). 'An empirical study of the behaviour of programs in a paging environment', *Ass. Comput. Mach. Symp. on Operating System Principles.*
Corbató, F.J., Daggett, M.M., and Daley, R.C. (1962). 'An experimental time-sharing system', *AFIPS Conference Proc.* **21**, 335.
Corbató, F.J., et al. (1965). *The Compatible Time-sharing System : a Programmer's Guide*, M.I.T. Press.
Corbató, F.J., and Vyssotsky, V.A. (1965). 'An introduction and overview of the MULTICS system', *AFIPS Conference Proc.*, **27**, 185.
Culler, G.J. (1966). *Culler On-line System* Univ. of California, Santa Barbara.
Daley, R.C., and Dennis, J.B. (1968). 'Virtual memory, processes and sharing in MULTICS', *Commons Ass. Comput. Mach.*, **11**, 306.
Daley, R.C., and Neumann, P.G. (1965). 'A general-purpose file system for secondary storage', *AFIPS Conference Proc.*, **27**, 213.
David, E.E., and Fano, R.M. (1965). 'Some thoughts about the social implications of accessible computing', *AFIPS Conference Proc.*, **27**, 243.
DEC (1968). 'Introduction to data communication', by Murphy, D.E. and Kallis, S.A.
Dennis, J.B. (1965). 'Segmentation and the design of multiprogrammed computer systems', *IEEE Int. Conv. Rec.*, **13**, 214.

Dennis, J.B. (1967). 'A position paper on computing and communication'. *Ass. Comput. Mach. Symp. on Operating System Principles.*
Dennis, J.B., and Glaser, E.L. (1965). 'The structure of on-line information processing systems', *Proc. 2nd Congr. Information System Sciences,* 1.
Dijkstra, E.W. (1967). 'The structure of the 'The'-multiprogramming system', *Ass. Comput. Mach. Symp. on Operating System Principles.*
Evans, D.C., and Leclerc, J.Y. (1967). 'Address mapping and the control of access in an interactive computer', *AFIPS Conference Proc.,* **30**, 23.
Fano, R.M. (1965). 'The MAC system; the computer utility approach', *IEEE Spectrum,* **2**, 56.
Fotheringham, J. (1961). 'Dynamic storage allocation in the Atlas computer, including an automatic use of backing store', *Commons Ass. Comput. Mach.,* **4**, 435.
Graham, R.M. (1968). 'Protection in an information processing utility', *Commons Ass. Comput. Mach.,* **11**, 365.
Huxtable, D.H.R., and Warwick, M.T. (1967). 'Dynamic supervisors—their design and construction', *Ass. Comput. Mach. Symp. on Operating System Principles.*
IBM (1966). 'System/360 Model 67. Time-sharing system. Preliminary technical summary'. Form C20-1647-0.
ICL (1968). 'Data communications and interogration', Form 4086.
Kerry, D.W. (1967). 'Choosing computers for the Post Office', *BCS Computer Bulletin,* **10**, No. 4, 12.
Kilburn, T., Payne, R.B., and Howarth, D.J. (1961). 'The Atlas Supervisor', AFIPS Conference Proc., **20**, 279.
Kurtz, T.E., and Lochner, K.M. (1965). 'Supervisory system for the Dartmouth time-sharing system', *Computers Automn,* **14**, No. 10, 25.
Lampson, B.W. (1968). 'A scheduling philosophy for multiprocessing systems', *Commons Ass. Comput. Mach.,* **11**, 347.
Licklider, J.C.R. (1965). 'Man-machine interaction : remote consoles and displays'. IFIP Congress 65 Proc., 504.
McCarthy, J., Boilen, S., Fredkin, E., and Licklider, J.C.R. (1963). 'A time-sharing debugging system for a small computer', AFIPS Conference Proc., **23**, 51.
Meredith Smith, J. (1968). 'A review and comparison of certain methods of computer performance evaluation', BCS Computer Bulletin 12, No. 1, 13.
Mullaney, F.C. (1965). 'Man-machine interaction : graphic data processing'. IFIP Congress 65 Proc., 578.
Oppenheimer, G., and Weizer, N. (1967). 'Resource management for a medium-scale time-sharing operating system'. *Ass. Comput. Mach. Symp. on Operating System Principles.*
O'Neill, R.W. (1967). 'Experience using a time-sharing, multiprogramming system with dynamic address relocation hardware'. AFIPS Conference Proc., **30**, 611.
Randell, B. and Kuehner, C.J. (1967). 'Dynamic storage allocation systems'. *Ass. Comput. Mach. Symp. on Operating System Principles.*
Smith, J.W. (1970). 'JOSS-II : design philosophy'. *A. Rev. Autom. Progmg.,* **6**, Pt 4, 183.
Van Horn, E.C. (1967). 'Three criteria for designing computing systems to facilitate debugging'. *Ass. Comput. Mach. Symp. on Operating System Principles.*
Vyssotsky, V.A., Corbató, F.J., and Graham, R.M. (1965). 'Structure of the MULTICS supervisor'. AFIPS Conference Proc., **27**, 203.
Wilkes, M.V. (1967). 'The design of multiple access computer systems', BCS Journal, **10**, No. 1, 1.

Wilkes and Needham, (1968). 'The design of multiple access computer systems', BCS Journal, **10**, No.4, 315.
Wilkes, M.V. (1968). *'Time-Sharing Computer Systems'*, Macdonald/Elsevier.

Index

accounting   106
AID   20
ALGOL   20
architechture — see system architechture
associative registers   82, 84
asynchronous line interface   61
asynchronous transmission   96–99
automatic telephone answering   65

background jobs   11, 48, 109
base-limit register   87
BASIC   23, 90
batch processing   3, 6, 42, 53
benchmark   117, 121
break point   35

character displays   38
COBOL   19
command languages   10–19
communication processor   62
communications   60–65
compiling   11, 89–92
console — see terminal
CTSS   107, 108

Dartmouth editor   30, 31
Dartmouth system   30
debugging aids   33–38
displays   38–40
duplex line   64
dynamic debugging   34–38, 90

editors   11, 28–33
executive — see supervisor

file,
-access   27, 28

-directories   25, 27
-manipulation   11
-sharing   26, 27
-security   25–28, 111–113
filing systems   25–28
foreground   48
FORTRAN   12

graphic displays   39

half duplex line   64
incremental dumping   111
installation   113–116
instruction set   92–93
interpreter   89–92
interrupts   66–73

job information block   75–76
job queues   75–76
JOSS   20, 35, 92

languages   19–25
light pen   39
limit register — see base-limit register
logging in   11

mapping   57
map registers   78–80
memory,
-allocation   54
-mapping   57, 78–80
-protection   54
monitor — see supervisor
MULTICS   85
multiplexer   60–61, 95–96
multiprogramming   1, 44, 49, 52–57, 66–73

139

operating systems   5–7

paging   57–60, 81–86, 110
programming languages   19–25
protection   111–113
pure code – see re-entrant code

real-time   1, 5
re-entrant code   51, 56, 86–89
relocation   54, 72–73
remote batch terminal   40
remote job entry   42–46
resource allocation   12, 103–106
response time   2
roll-in/roll-out   46–52

scheduling   45, 53, 74, 106–111
segmentation   83–85
selector   74
sharable code – see re-entrant
simplex line   64
spooling   44
state   69, 70
state word   79, 84

supervisor   66–73
supervisor call (SVC)   66–73
SVC – see supervisor call
swapping   51, 52–57, 74–78
swapping channel   56
swapping device   51
synchronous line interface   99–102
synchronous transmission   61
system architechture   92–95

TELCOMP   35
Teletype   38
terminal devices   38–41
text editor   31
time-sharing   1, 7
time slice   46, 51, 52, 74–78
trace   35
trusted program   88

uniprogramming   43
user mode   69

virtual memory   82

Printed in Great Britain
by Alden & Mowbray Ltd.
at the Alden Press, Oxford.

QA
76.5
B816

DEC 4 1972